Available Titles

 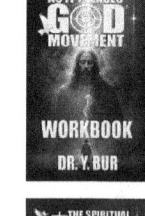   

ASITPLEASESGOD.COM

CREATIVE MINDSET
As It Pleases God®

Copyright © 2024 by R.O.A.R. Publishing Group. All rights reserved.

Visit www.DrYBur.com or www.AsItPleasesGod.com for more information. No part of this publication may be reproduced, stored in a retrieval system, or transmitted in any way by any means, electronic, mechanical, photocopy, recording, or otherwise, without the prior permission of the author, except as provided by USA copyright law. All rights reserved.

R.O.A.R. Publishing Group
581 N. Park Ave. Ste. #725
Apopka, FL 32704
ROAR-58-2316
762-758-2316
www.RoarPublishingGroup.com

AIPG Donation Link

Scan to Pay

Published in the United States of America
ISBN: 978-1-948936-94-1
$22.88

ASITPLEASESGOD.COM

Send AS IT PLEASES GOD

Book Series **and** *Workbook* **Testimonies, Donations, or Orders to**

Dr. Y. Bur
R.O.A.R. Publishing Group
581 N. Park Ave. Ste. #725
Apopka, FL 32704
ROAR-58-2316
762-758-2316
📧 Dr.YBur@gmail.com

Visit Us At:

 AsItPleasesGodMovement

 AsItPleasesGod

🖥 DrYBur.com
🖥 AsItPleasesGod.com

Please Donate

Please DONATE to this *Missionable Movement of God* as a GIVE-BACK to the Kingdom. Thanks for your support. Many Blessings.

AIPG Donation Link

Scan to Pay

Table of Contents

Introduction 11
Chapter 1 17
   Cutting Through the Red Tape 17
      Counteracting Negativity 20
      Workmanship 23
Chapter 2 25
   Balancing Act 25
      Kingdom Documentation 27
      Rejecting Divine Knowledge and Wisdom 31
      The Proof Is In The Pudding 33
      Scarcity Mindset 37
Chapter 3 43
   Spiritual Side-Eye 43
      Shamefulness 47
      Spiritual Levels 50
Chapter 4 53
   Hidden Hustle 53
      Deep Calleth To The Deep 59
      Raising Questions 64
Chapter 5 69
   Authentically Creative 69

Divine Illumination 74

Creative Characteristics 77

Chapter 6 83

Divine Paper Trail 83

Chapter 7 89

Creative Mindset 89

Building Upward 93

Spiritual Respect 98

Chapter 8 103

Fruit Inspection 103

Love Inspection 105

Joy Inspection 109

Peace Inspection 112

Patience Inspection 117

Kindness Inspection 121

Goodness Inspection 126

Faithfulness Inspection 130

Gentleness Inspection 135

Self-Control Inspection 137

The Use of Spiritual Fruits 140

Chapter 9 145

Work-In-Progress Mentality 145

Words in Progress 147

Touch of Progress 150

Approach to Progress 153

Thoughts of Progress 155

Respect for Progress 158
Trusting The Process 162

Chapter 10 167
Take Risks 167
Divine Wisdom, Understanding, and Guidance 170
The Divine Print 171
Power of Repentant Forgiveness 173

Chapter 11 183
Joint Ventures 183
Harmonious Love 184
Spirit of Humility and Servant Leadership 190
The Bonding Factors 191
Dualism of Envy and Jealousy 193

Chapter 12 201
Creative Playbook 201
Spiritual Ammunition 206
Zip Your Lips 210

INTRODUCTION

Are you tired of feeling left behind while trying too hard to catch up? Are you fed up with lacking originality and underhandedly sucker-punching those who do? Is your imagination locked in a buffering state? Then again, are you looking for the forward-thinking innovation that you have yet to find in anyone, anything, or with nothing? Look no further, as the Creative Mindset, *As It Pleases God*, can help you unleash your full potential and bring out the creativity that lies within you!

The groundbreaking or brainstorming mindset that you are looking to develop is grafted into the pages of this *Creative Playbook* for a time such as this. Life has served you enough lemons; it is time to own a chain of lemonade stands. Why not just make lemonade with the lemons? You have the free will to do so if you like. But let me be the first to say, 'With a little *Fruit Inspection*, mediocrity is not your portion...Greatness is your BIRTHRIGHT!'

The most sought-after and coveted state of being is a Creative Mindset, which we already possess but fail to understand how to gain access to. In the Eye of God, creativity has nothing to do with smarts, aptitude, intellectualism, status, fame, fortune, rhyme, or reason. However, those things may help us in the commission of its use or the capitalization process.

Still, they do not get your mental wheels turning, *As It Pleases God* and according to your Predestined Blueprint. Nor do they give leeway to opt out of charactorial development or permit an excuse not to revamp flawed people skills. What is the big deal in this matter? The deal is: To embrace the Creative Characteristics that will put your enemies to boot, you must behave according to Kingdom Standards to Spiritually Glean the Divine Creativity that is already yours.

Is God behaving fairly by withholding what is already ours? It depends on the perception of the rescinding factors, the violated contingencies, the readiness or traumatization involved, or whether we are selfishly pleasing ourselves over Him. But know this: *"Many are the plans in a person's heart, but it is the Lord's purpose that prevails."* Proverbs 19:21.

Regardless of how we feel about the withholding process, our Blueprinted Mission takes precedence over how we feel, think, plan, believe, or behave, invoking a Rod of Correction or Spiritual Classroom for all mankind. Really? Yes, really! *"In their hearts humans plan their course, but the Lord establishes their steps."* Proverbs 16:9. It is always best to approach any plan of action, *As It Pleases God*. Besides, it will help us in the long run more than it will bring harm to us. Here is the Spiritual Seal: " *'For I know the plans I have for you,' declares the Lord, 'plans to prosper you and not to harm you, plans to give you hope and a future.'* " Jeremiah 29:11.

Now, if we are in fear or do not trust God, all we need to do is repeat Jeremiah 29:11 or write it on the plan before handing it over to Him. Why must we repeat or document this scripture as Believers? First, it aids in getting out of our own way while helping us to develop faith from the inside out. Secondly, it assists in aligning ourselves, *As It Pleases Him*, because *"The Lord foils the plans of the nations; he thwarts the purposes of the peoples."* Psalm 33:10.

What if we are already creative and do not need anyone's help in this matter? Our level of creativity is a matter of perception. Keep in mind that no one is creative at everything, and if we do not know the reason for our being, *As It Pleases God*, we may be operating in a deficit from the inside out to mask what we do not know. Then again, we may use superficial creativity or knowledge to hide the underlying truth about ourselves. Otherwise, we may whitewash the fact that we lack authentic wisdom.

How do we make wisdom make sense? Wisdom does not need to make sense; instead, it gives us common sense amid nonsense and folly. Here is the deal: According to the Heavenly of Heavens, the critical stage of fundamental wisdom, *As It Pleases God*, takes your average whatever to above average. And then, with discipline, it takes your good to better, your better to best, and your best to the greatest. Regardless of which stage you are in, know this: *"Wisdom is the principal thing; Therefore, get wisdom. And in all your getting, get understanding."* Proverbs 4:7.

Without wisdom and understanding, we can operate in a deficit, Mentally, Physically, Emotionally, or Spiritually, without knowing it. Then again, we may confuse knowledge with wisdom and wisdom with knowledge without understanding the *Balancing Act* needed to allow them to succinctly work together when *Cutting Through The Red Tape*. Here is what Proverbs 19:8 shares with us: *"He who gets wisdom loves his own soul; He who keeps understanding will find good."* Here is a list of examples to help understand ordinary wisdom, but not limited to such:

- ☐ Wisdom helps us make better decisions.
- ☐ It allows us to see things from different perspectives.
- ☐ Wisdom helps us understand ourselves better.
- ☐ It helps us deal with difficult emotions and situations.
- ☐ Wisdom helps us build better relationships.

- ☐ It helps us set a guard over our tongues.
- ☐ Wisdom helps us become more compassionate.
- ☐ It helps us become more patient and understanding.
- ☐ Wisdom allows us to appreciate the simple things.
- ☐ It helps us find meaning and purpose.
- ☐ It allows us to lead a more fulfilling and satisfying life.
- ☐ Wisdom helps us achieve our goals and dreams.
- ☐ It helps us become more resilient and grateful.
- ☐ Wisdom allows us to learn from our mistakes.
- ☐ It helps us become more creative and innovative.
- ☐ It allows us to see the world in a more positive light.
- ☐ Wisdom helps us become more responsible.
- ☐ It helps us become better leaders and role models.
- ☐ Wisdom enables us to contribute to society.
- ☐ It helps us leave a positive legacy for future generations.
- ☐ Wisdom helps us live a life without regret.
- ☐ It helps us grow as individuals.
- ☐ Wisdom helps us navigate our perceptions.

Ordinary wisdom and Supernatural Wisdom are not the same, but you will learn the difference a little later in this book. So, you want to make sure that you do not miss out on this sought-after information to benefit your Heaven on Earth Experience.

Unfortunately, with wisdom or not, most issues you face today are derived from a lack of understanding or the lack of being understood, in conjunction with the words that you use to connect them both. Whether your words are good, bad, indifferent, or considered a word salad, this combination will either make you or break you in the Eye of God. Really? Yes, really! *"He who has knowledge spares his words, And a man of understanding is of a calm spirit."* Proverbs 17:27.

The bottom line is that a word check-up is needed when dealing with knowledge, wisdom, and understanding. Why is word governing crucial? Words bridge the positive or negative gaps in your Creative Mindset, building and burning bridges as well. According to the Heavenly of Heavens, remote-control words are not going to get it in the Eye of God. What does this mean in layman's terms? Unfortunately, using remote controls or robotic words leaves room for error, jamming, folly, and mischief, which can hurt innocent people. Thus, by using the Word of God and the Fruits of the Spirit to foolproof, deprogram, or de-jam unwise words, building bridges will become a part of a Creative Portfolio of Greatness, primarily if our reason for being is known.

Now, if you DO NOT know your reason for being, then it behooves you to read this book from cover to cover to bring forth what you never knew existed within you. According to the Heavenly of Heavens, if your resourcefulness is not resourced or *Raising Questions*, it is time to restrategize your approach to God, yourself, and others. Your *Authentically Creative* DESTINY is riding on your coattail, waiting for you to do something about it. You know it, your psyche knows it, and your conscience keeps nudging you!

With a *Work-In-Progress Mentality*, all you need is a plan that aligns with your natural capabilities, possessing the hidden reservoir of ingenuity to avoid getting a *Spiritual Side-Eye* from your Heavenly Father. For this reason, this book is designed to give the one-up or the rundown on the *Hidden Hustle*, taking your mind from mediocrity to doing what you never thought you were able to do with endless possibilities.

Now, the most ingenious question is, 'Are you willing to *Take Risks* for your Creative Mindset?' Better yet, 'Are you willing to step out of your comfort zone and embrace change to unleash your creativity?' If your answer is a resounding yes, then this book is undoubtedly meant for you.

On the other hand, if the answer is no, declining risk and change, then it is advisable not to waste your precious time gleaning without execution. Remember, time is a valuable commodity, and it is crucial to use it wisely. So, it is better to focus your efforts on something that will yield results instead of wasting your precious time and energy on frivolity.

As Dr. Y. Bur, the WHY Doctor, I am here to challenge you, and if you are not prepared to up the ante on your Creative Mindset and Skills, then our *Joint Venture* will not serve its purpose, *As It Pleases God*. Why? Simply put, for a time such as this, RENEWAL is a must. Romans 12:2 says, *"And do not be conformed to this world, but be transformed by the renewing of your mind, that you may prove what is that good and acceptable and perfect will of God."*

In this book, I will share the inside information on how to gain Divine Access from the Heavenly of Heavens to break yokes, sever soul ties, and set captives free, Mentally, Physically, Emotionally, and Spiritually. So, if you are ready to put on your thinking cap, let us jump in, getting both feet WET with the FIREPOWER from Isaiah 43:2: *"When you pass through the waters, I will be with you; And through the rivers, they shall not overflow you. When you walk through the fire, you shall not be burned, Nor shall the flame scorch you."*

Chapter 1
Cutting Through the Red Tape

At some point in our lives, we will find ourselves Cutting Through The Red Tape when embarking upon a Spiritual Journey with God. In this transformative experience or place, some survive, some avoid it, some hide, and others give up. Then again, some allow themselves to become bogged down with the issues, distractions, busyness, and obstacles that prevent them from fully embracing their Spiritual Journey or Divine Blueprint. Nor do they allow themselves to develop a Creative Mindset, taking them from where they are to their NEXT. Regardless of whether this is you or someone you may know, in this chapter, we will explore some ways to Cut Through The Red Tape and how to stay focused, *As It Pleases God.*

A Creative Mindset is a Heavenly Commodity granted to all and used only by a few. For this reason, now is the time to UNVEIL what is already within, to bring us in Purpose on purpose, and do what we have been created to do, *As It Pleases God.* Many of us do not realize the potential that lies within us while having googly eyes or coveting those who appear better, stronger, or wiser, but leading us straight into the PIT of idolatry.

Then again, we get caught up in our daily routines and forget to take the time to be effortlessly creative or grateful, and we also forget to incorporate Spiritual Principles. As a result, we let fear, anger, hatred, biases, resentment, conditioning, peer pressure, unforgiveness, and self-doubt hold us back from exploring our ideas and bringing them to life, doing what we were called to do, or being about our Father's Business, *As It Pleases Him.*

As we cut through the Spiritual Red Tape for a time such as this, we now have the opportunity to change the trajectory of this malevolent mindset that is zapping our Divine Creativity. Why is it malevolent, especially as Believers doing our best and loving God with all our hearts? First, we were all created with a Predestined Purpose and Blueprint. When operating outside of this safe zone, we subject ourselves to malevolency with or without our permission by reason of omission. Simply put, for not knowing our reason for being or operating in cluelessness, opting to do what we want, when, how, why, and with whomever, with God nowhere in sight, *As It Pleases Him,* we can become yoked, soul-tied, and oppressed from the inside out.

Secondly, as a part of this process, we must use our Creative Minds to make a difference in the world for the Greater Good, not for the lesser agendas with selfish attachments or unworthy benefits. Plus, it becomes malevolent when we knowingly or unknowingly hide our Spiritual Tools. On the contrary, we may also use them for debauchery to turn on ourselves or oppress others while appearing right or justified in our own eyes.

How do we break malevolency, turning it into benevolence? We must get an understanding from a Kingdom Perspective, *As It Pleases God.* When seeking to PLEASE Him, malevolency involves harboring evil or malicious intent, engaging in debaucherous or destructive behavior, and deviating from the moral and ethical standards established by our Heavenly Father.

According to the Heavenly of Heavens, it is crucial to embody kindness, love, peace, patience, goodness, gentleness, faithfulness, joy, and self-control while behaving Christlike. Unbeknown to most, when refraining from malevolent actions, beliefs, desires, and thoughts, we have a better chance of Counteracting Negativity at the drop of a dime. Plus, in the Eye of God, we should NEVER allow our malevolency to evolve into a few items, but not limited to such:

- ☐ Rebellion.
- ☐ Folly.
- ☐ Ungratefulness.
- ☐ Haughtiness.
- ☐ Waywardness.
- ☐ Revenge.
- ☐ Stiffneckness.
- ☐ Dullness.
- ☐ Unforgiveness.
- ☐ Hatefulness.
- ☐ Recklessness.
- ☐ Lukewarmness.

Why do we need an avoidance checklist as Believers? On our Spiritual Journey, we will encounter situations, circumstances, events, and people that test our patience, kindness, and integrity. Frankly, it is during these challenging times that our true character is revealed, and whether or not the Spiritual Principles of Righteousness, Fairness, and Justice guide us.

Now, regardless of where we are or where we fall on the scale, good, bad, or indifferent, we all have the RIGHT to Counteract Negativity or prevent it from taking root. Doing so helps to avoid its repercussions, erosion of trust, breakdown of relationships, violating our integrity, treading a dangerous path, or compromising our values, to name a few.

Counteracting Negativity

According to the Heavenly of Heavens, we must counteract all negative characteristics with the Word of God, repentance, forgiveness, gratefulness, mercifulness, and prayerfulness. At the same time, we must also cover them all with the Blood of Jesus as a form of Spiritual Atonement or Seal.

Why must we go through all of these steps to counteract negativity? Unfortunately, negativity has a way of coming for us, even if we do not want it. So, we must reject or resist it. 1 Peter 5:8-9 says, *"Be sober, be vigilant; because your adversary the devil walks about like a roaring lion, seeking whom he may devour. Resist him, steadfast in the faith, knowing that the same sufferings are experienced by your brotherhood in the world."*

What if we do not resist negativity? We have free will to accept or resist it, them, or that. Still, by not resisting negativity, it is as if we are giving it silent permission, or we are coming into an agreement by not saying anything. *"Therefore submit to God. Resist the devil and he will flee from you."* James 4:7. When rejecting negativity, we do not need to become combative, loud, rude, or pretentious. Just reverse it kindly and smoothly, like honey dripping from a honeycomb.

For example, if someone says, 'You are unattractive to me.' I would say, 'I am beautiful in the Eye of God. Thus, He makes everything beautiful in its Divine Timing, and He does not make mistakes.' In closing, I would wrap up my response with an open-ended redirecting question of concern provoking the element of thought, such as: 'What do you think about how God sees beauty?' 'How do you feel about God's beauty residing from the inside out?' Or, then again, I may flip the script by asking, 'Would you agree?'

What is the purpose of gaining agreement in the reversal, canceling, or counteracting? Once the negative forecaster comes into agreement with our positive reversal, it creates a double-seal. How so? They came into agreement with the positivity that we interjected to intercept their debaucherous attempts. With this approach, more than likely, they will move on to an easier victim. What if they do not? Unfortunately, they will begin to turn on themselves from the inside out with all types of insecurities and negative mental chatter. Remember this: *"A gentle answer turns away wrath, but a harsh word stirs up anger."* Proverbs 15:1.

Here is what I know beyond a shadow of a doubt when canceling, rejecting, or reversing pessimistic forecasts attacking me, my fruitful inner beauty, or my Creative Mindset. 2 Corinthians 10:4-5 says, *"For the weapons of our warfare are not carnal but mighty in God for pulling down strongholds, casting down arguments and every high thing that exalts itself against the knowledge of God, bringing every thought into captivity to the obedience of Christ."*

How is 2 Corinthians 10:4-5 applicable to Believers? For example, being that I am in Purpose on purpose with my Divine Blueprint in hand for the Kingdom, As It Pleases God, using the Fruits of the Spirit and behaving Christlike, I can legally pull down a stronghold. Due to the Blood of Jesus, I have the Spiritual Right to shut hostile opposing forces down, period! Then, keep it moving in the Spirit of Excellence with a work-in-progress mentality, being about my Father's Business.

In all simplicity, we cannot behave like the stronghold that we are pulling down. Why can we not treat others like they are treating us, especially when it is harmful, rude, abusive, or demeaning? In the Realm of the Spirit, it is a double-negative with zero sparks or firepower when misbehaving. Plus, behaving like them has a mirror attached, reflecting whatever we do, say, or become, positively or negatively. Here is what James 1:23-25 says about this matter: *"For if anyone is a hearer of the word and not a doer, he is like a man observing his natural face in a mirror; for he observes himself, goes away, and immediately forgets what kind of man he was. But he who looks into the perfect law of liberty and* continues in it, and is not a forgetful hearer but a doer of the work, this one will be blessed in what he does."

When dealing with a Creative Mindset, we must become a MASTER at the reversal process, creating a win-win out of everything and with everyone, regardless of how it appears to the naked eye. *"Let us search out and examine our ways, and turn back to the Lord."* Lamentations 3:40.

Why must we counteract negativity with positivity? First, it helps us resist the enemy who tries to distort our minds or plant seeds of negativity and debauchery. Simply put, we must proactively uproot, doing our due diligence before God steps into the matter. Will God really step into a matter we refuse to deal with? Absolutely! *"But He answered and said, 'Every plant which My heavenly Father has not planted will be uprooted.'"* Matthew 15:13. By counteracting as such, it regulates our minds back into the Will or Word of God with humility before He starts pruning. *"For I say, through the grace given to me, to everyone who is among you, not to think of himself more highly than he ought to think, but to think soberly, as God has dealt to each one a measure of faith."* Romans 12:3.

Secondly, it assists in seeing ourselves or our heart postures clearly. *"As in water face reflects face, so a man's heart reveals the man."* Proverbs 27:19. Reflecting in such a manner helps us to determine which Fruits of the Spirit we need to use to prevent Spiritual Blindness, Deafness, or Muteness. In addition, it also safeguards us from falling into our own self-created or self-induced ditches. Here is the warning: *"Behold, the wicked brings forth iniquity; Yes, he conceives trouble and brings forth falsehood. He made a pit and dug it out, And has fallen into the ditch which he made. His trouble shall return upon his own head, And his violent dealing shall come down on his own crown."* Psalm 7:14-16.

Thirdly, it promotes self-correction or self-analysis automatically within the human psyche, regulating our internal compass. Then again, it allows the conscience to kick in, nudging our senses and sending red flags to do or say the right things, *As It Pleases God.* "Let nothing be done through selfish ambition or conceit, but in lowliness of mind let each esteem others better than himself. Let each of you look out not only for his own interests, but also for the interests of others." Philippians 2:3-4.

Fourthly, it helps us to become content with who we are from the inside out while becoming a work-in-progress, *As It Pleases God.* Nevertheless, in doing so, "Let each one examine his own work, and then he will have rejoicing in himself alone, and not in another." Galatians 6:4.

Workmanship

In Cutting Through the Red Tape, we are the Workmanship of the Kingdom of God. Therefore, we must awaken from our slumber to understand the differences we face in today's day and age in working on ourselves for ourselves, working on ourselves according to the Will of God, or working on ourselves to prove something to others. By knowing why we do what we do and why we are not doing what we should, we gain a better understanding of the good and bad residing within us all.

Malevolency and benevolence are essential in understanding the relationship between our human nature and DIVINE NATURE, especially when dealing with a Creative Mindset. The tendency to do evil or cause harm is within everyone, even if we pretend to be a saint.

For example, if someone tries to woo me with perfection or the persona that they would not hurt a fly, I do not trust them at all! Why is trust not extended? We all have this one thing called a SURVIVAL INSTINCT, and once it kicks in, we do not know what we will or will not do until we are placed in that position.

Imagine a scenario where a person who is starving receives a meal from a kind-hearted individual. However, while they are trying to consume the meal, a fly hovers around their food, threatening to lay eggs in it. In the face of this adversity, what do you think the individual would do in such a situation? My point exactly! They will take the fly out by any means necessary to survive until the next meal.

Plus, regardless of how we feel about God's Divine Approach or Method of Operation, PRESSURE is how He tests the best of the best and the worst of the worst to get the oil to flow, *As It Pleases Him*, bringing forth the crème de la crème. Then again, it may be His way of pumping the brakes on us, them, or that, due to some form of self-pleasure, self-aggrandizement, misuse, abuse, ungratefulness, or outright selfishness. All in all, I want to see how an individual operates under pressure to determine the posture of their mindset, thought set, word set, focus set, heart set, and people skills.

On the other hand, or better yet, on the opposite side of the spectrum, when dealing with malevolency and benevolence, we all have the tendency to do good. Whether we engage in goodness is a matter of choice, but rest assured, it is there. It may be cemented or buried, but God will always give us something good to work with. Unbeknown to most, the two create BALANCE in the Eye of God, allowing us the free will to CHOOSE which side we lean toward and recognize the differences between the two.

Although sometimes it may appear as if we are engaging in a Balancing Act for the sake of the Kingdom, God understands because we have the right to feel how we feel. Sometimes, we get stuck in our own ways of thinking and can become closed off to new possibilities. Nonetheless, by staying open and curious, *As It Pleases God*, we can continue to grow and evolve on our Spiritual Journey, regardless of the nay-sayers, dream killers, or player-haters.

Chapter 2

Balancing Act

Do you feel as if you are imbalanced? Are you feeling wishy-washy in your decision-making process? Do you know someone who is struggling to find balance? Is juggling multiple passions and responsibilities getting the best of you? Then again, are you ready to just unplug due to extreme exhaustion? If so, you are not alone. Life is designed to introduce Seasons and Vicissitudes into our lives to shake us up or humble us down to the core. In the Balancing Act, the key is to know the differences while learning and growing through them, *As It Pleases God*.

Building a Spiritual Relationship with God can be a challenging but rewarding experience. Nevertheless, when building *Spirit to Spirit* Relations, *As It Pleases Him* requires a delicate Balancing Act between devotion, faith, prayer, forgiveness, mercy, repentance, understanding, and trainability. I understand there seem to be a lot of things to do to maintain balance, but they are all doable. Here is what James 4:8 tells us to do: *"Draw near to God and He will draw near to you. Cleanse your hands, you sinners; and purify your hearts, you double-minded."*

What if we are not double-minded? Once again, this is how we are deceived. We all have the potential to become double-minded from time to time, especially when the WHY factor is missing. However, the goal is never to remain in this state by getting an understanding or asking the right fact-finding questions about the duality. For this reason, we have the Word of God as a roadmap, the Blood of Jesus to cover us, the Holy Spirit to guide us, and the Fruits of the Spirit to invoke Christlike Characteristics for our Heaven on Earth Experiences, making the Balancing Act balanced.

Suppose we utilize the Fruits of the Spirit to establish usable Christlike Character in our Balancing Acts. In this case, it becomes easier to cultivate a strong sense of devotion and reverence towards God, our Heavenly Father.

When aligning our lives with His Divine Will by making God a central focal point, He will move Heaven and Earth on our behalf. According to the Ancient of Days, in the Balancing Act of mankind, we must become ever so mindful about our thoughts, words, reactions, and deeds. More importantly, we have a second step associated with being mindful as such. We must align them with Spiritual Principles of love, compassion, growth, selflessness, and change, building a solid foundation for the Greater Good, *As It Pleases Him*.

Why must we add a second step to the Balancing Act as Believers? First, God did not create us as robots or animals, nor should we behave as such. Secondly, He has set higher expectations for us; thus, He has given us the ability to communicate and convey effectively to carry out this task. Clearly, no one is perfect or flawless, but we must strive towards PLEASING God and aligning with His Divine Will to unveil our Predestined Blueprint and Spiritual Gifts.

In any event, without balance, we will fall short in the Eye of God in due season. To take this a step further, without balance, we cannot walk a straight line; without balance, the psyche will have us for lunch; without balance, our minds will have a field day with our emotions; without balance, we cannot see our way clearly through the Vicissitudes and Cycles of Life, provoking self-correction with an attempt to heal itself.

Nevertheless, when pressed with a Balancing Act as such, here are a few questions to consider: *"Do you know when God dispatches them, And causes the light of His cloud to shine? Do you know how the clouds are balanced, Those wondrous works of Him who is perfect in knowledge? Why are your garments hot, When He quiets the earth by the south wind? With Him, have you spread out the skies, Strong as a cast metal mirror? 'Teach us what we should say to Him, For we can prepare nothing because of the darkness.' "* Job 37:15-19.

Why must we question ourselves amid our darkest moments? Please allow me to answer this question with another: 'How can we obtain answers and solutions without querying ourselves?' Engaging in the Balancing Act, *As It Pleases God*, we must become excellent at asking questions and documenting answers. If we do not like being questioned, we will experience insurmountable difficulty on our Spiritual Journey. What is more, if we do not like documenting, we will experience more hardship than those who document instructions, lessons, ideas, thoughts, and so on to reflect.

Why would this happen to us, especially if we do not like documenting or we do not have time to do so? In today's fast-paced world, time is of the utmost importance. We all have deadlines to meet, meetings to attend, tasks to complete, and families to attend to. In such a scenario, documenting important information might seem like an added burden or may seem a little hideous. However, avoiding documentation can prove to be counterproductive in the long run, especially when omitting Kingdom Documentation.

Kingdom Documentation

We often view Kingdom Documentation as a grueling task, but I must say that it is the most liberating one. Because *"All Scripture is given by inspiration of God, and is profitable for doctrine, for reproof, for correction, for instruction in righteousness."* 2 Timothy

3:16. What does this scripture have to do with anything? If we take a moment to document and answer questions from this particular scripture, we will always have something to document. Here are a few underlying questions, but not limited to such.

- ☐ What was the inspiration that originated from God?
- ☐ How does God inspire us through this?
- ☐ What did we learn from God?
- ☐ How did we learn from Him?
- ☐ What correction occurred?
- ☐ Why did the correction occur?
- ☐ How did we become a better person because of this?
- ☐ What is our give-back as a result of this situation?
- ☐ How did we apply the Fruits of the Spirit?
- ☐ How does this make us more Christlike?
- ☐ What is the win-win?
- ☐ How can we use this for the Greater Good?

Can these questions really get the ball rolling on our documenting forum? Absolutely! These are trigger questions derived from the Word of God, and if we engage in *Spirit to Spirit* Relations *As It Pleases Him,* the Voice from Within will speak loudly. But, of course, only loud enough for us to hear.

What if we omit documenting? We have free will to do whatever we like to do; however, to avoid documenting is like having to ask a person repeatedly for the same information. It not only wastes your time but also the time of the person you are asking for information that you failed to document. Moreover, it can lead to misunderstandings, avoidance, and confusion, causing people to withhold information, especially in a professional setting. In addition, it creates an unprofessional image, disrespectfulness, and folly on our behalf, leading to frustration and loss of trust and credibility.

Then again, refusing to document can create a bottleneck in workflows, leading to delays, omitted information, or missed deadlines. Thus, the same applies to the Realm of the Spirit. Habakkuk 2:2 says, *"Then the Lord answered me and said: 'Write the vision And make it plain on tablets, That he may run who reads it.'"* So, the next time you are tempted to skip documenting important information, remember that in the Balancing Act, it takes less energy to document it and be done, moving on to the next thing. Isaiah 30:8 says, *"Now go, write it before them on a tablet, And note it on a scroll, That it may be for time to come, Forever and ever."*

What is the big deal about documenting? If we want the enemy to steal our dreams or the information we hear quickly, just refuse to document...the information will find wings to leave or become choked by thorns. Please allow me to Spiritually Align: *"And some seed fell among thorns, and the thorns sprang up and choked them. But others fell on good ground and yielded a crop: some a hundredfold, some sixty, some thirty. He who has ears to hear, let him hear!"* Matthew 13:7-9.

On the other hand, let me put my spin on this matter: 'He who has a hand, let him write!' If we establish a Spiritual Journal or Reference Log, we can reflect, revamp, restore, renew, regraft, or re-whatever. Here is the Spiritual Seal we can bank on: *"Most assuredly, I say to you, unless a grain of wheat falls into the ground and dies, it remains alone; but if it dies, it produces much grain."* John 12:24. How do we make this make sense? The documented seed can reproduce when it becomes a part of the page or is planted on the page that it is documented on. Without documentation, one must question, 'Where is the seed?'

Although Seedtime and Harvest may seem a little cliché, a documented seed in or out of season holds more potential than one that is never documented. How so? When our documentation is used in conjunction with patiently waiting, as stated in Isaiah 40:31, the underlying potential is exemplified. It says, *"But those who wait on the Lord shall renew their strength; They shall mount up with wings like eagles, They shall run and not be weary, They shall walk and not faint."*

Since everyone has a story to tell, from Genesis to Revelation of their lives, there should be a paper trail. Here is what we must know in the Balancing Act from John: *"I was in the Spirit on the Lord's Day, and I heard behind me a loud voice, as of a trumpet, saying, 'I am the Alpha and the Omega, the First and the Last,' and, 'What you see, write in a book and send it to the seven churches which are in Asia: to Ephesus, to Smyrna, to Pergamos, to Thyatira, to Sardis, to Philadelphia, and to Laodicea.'"* Revelation 1:11.

Unbeknown to most, the Vision or Predestined Blueprint for our lives also uses the Word of God and our Testimony of Jesus Christ, as John used to write the riveting Book of Revelation. Every human life will have ups and downs, right and wrongs, wins and losses, love and hate, trauma and healing, and so on. Still, it does not negate the sharing of lessons, devout understandings, gleaned knowledge, and enhanced wisdom.

If we do not document to our brothers, sisters, companions, children, friends, and foes as John did, then what are we doing? What lessons are we leaving behind? What did we learn in this lifetime that could help the next person? If the Writers of the Ancient had not taken the time to write or document their *Spirit to Spirit* Communion or Encounters with God, do we think we would have the Bible?

On this note, you are your own unique Book of the Bible. After all, no one can tell your story better than you. Blasphemy, right? Wrong! Here is the deal: Revelation 1:19 says, *"Write the things which you have seen, and the things which are, and the things which will take place after this."* If we think this does not apply to us, we are sadly mistaken. If we are not upholding our side of the Spiritual Agreement or Findings for our Heaven on Earth Experience, then one must ask, 'Are we living in vain?'

What if we feel unusable? A feeling is not a fact, nor is it an absolute. *"Do not be deceived, God is not mocked; for whatever a man sows, that he will also reap."* Galatians 6:7. All God needs is a WILLING SPIRIT with a selfless work-in-progress mentality, *As It Pleases Him*. Simply put, if we selflessly work on ourselves, we will reap the harvest. If we do not work on ourselves and become selfish, prideful, arrogant, rude, and disobedient with a reprobate mind, we will reap that harvest as well. Is this Biblical? *"And even as they did not like to retain God in their knowledge, God gave them over to a debased mind, to do those things which are not fitting."* Romans 1:28.

Rejecting Divine Knowledge and Wisdom

The consequences of rejecting God's Divine Knowledge and Wisdom are more common than we think or care to believe. Although we have free will, when we turn away from God Almighty, we also turn on ourselves. Most often, we turn on ourselves without knowing it until the full manifestation, yoke, soul-tie, or bondage occurs.

Why would we turn on ourselves as Believers sold out to the Kingdom of God? Just as God is Spirit, so are we. According to the Heavenly of Heavens, this is why *Spirit to Spirit* Relations work best for us instead of a Spirit to self, self to self, or self to another.

Without a *Spirit to Spirit* Connection, *As It Pleases God*, we become susceptible to experiencing a state of moral and Spiritual decline from the inside out. What does this mean? Before the physical manifestation takes place, it has already occurred within the psyche. We often tiptoe around this issue when Rejecting Divine Knowledge and Wisdom because the core of our being knows the truth. Yet, we often opt to lie to ourselves about our condition, or it is deflected onto others, without proper Spiritual Discernment.

Unfortunately, this misgoverning or rejecting trifecta gives birth to a distorted and thwarted understanding. In addition, it also leaves room for playing mind games, manipulating, or bullying to extract information based on our Spiritual Condition. What is the trifecta:

- ☐ Rejection of Knowledge.
- ☐ Rejection of Wisdom.
- ☐ Rejection of Spiritual Discernment.

Whenever we think we have the one-up on someone or something without Divine Knowledge, Divine Wisdom, and Spiritual Discernment, *As It Pleases God*, our right can be wrong, or our wrong can be correct in the Eye of God.

For example, if we think we are unusable, we may feel that we are correct from our perspective. Meanwhile, from God's Divine Perspective, we are all usable, and He will use anything or anyone to accomplish His Divine Will. Here again, if we think we are usable, we are correct from our perspective. But God sees us as an eyesore because we are disobedient, unforgiving, rude, and hateful.

In the Balancing Act, we can choose our hard! Nevertheless, we must also understand that without Spiritual Discernment, *As It Pleases God*, the mind can create whatever we want, what we are accustomed to, or whatever we relate back to. In all simplicity, this is similar to the word Religio, where we derive Religion (what we relate back to) to justify a means to an end, especially when a complete understanding is not established with the correct knowledge and wisdom on a lower level. Keep in mind, if we do not master lower-level knowledge and wisdom, we cannot master Divine Knowledge and Wisdom from the Heavenly of Heavens.

Here is the Spiritual Seal that we can capitalize on to make reaping and sowing beneficial: *"But you shall receive power when the Holy Spirit has come upon you; and you shall be witnesses to Me in Jerusalem, and in all Judea and Samaria, and to the end of the earth."* Acts 1:8.

Ephesians 6:11-12 shares what is needed of us; it says, *"Put on the whole armor of God, that you may be able to stand against the wiles of the devil. For we do not wrestle against flesh and blood, but against principalities, against powers, against the rulers of the darkness of this age, against spiritual hosts of wickedness in the heavenly places."* Here is my question: 'If we do not suit up with the Whole Armor of God, then what are we suiting up with?' Wait, wait, wait, do not answer this question yet! Let us go deeper...

The Proof Is In The Pudding

We can attempt to take the Balancing Acts of God as a joke. But when the joke is on us, then what do we do? Do we cry wolf? Do we play the victim? Do we project, deflect, reject, or reflect? Or do we assume responsibility? Regardless of our decisions, thoughts, or beliefs, it does not negate the fact that His Divine Calculations are connected to our Creative Mindsets or the Creative Juices that He ushers in. Nonetheless, the Proof Is In The Pudding.

What does pudding have to do with our Balancing Acts or Creative Mindsets? Pudding is an analogy used for holding or gelling things together for a delectable outcome. What if we do not like pudding? Then, think about this as the Law of Gravity...there is a Divine Force keeping us earthbound and not airborne unless superseded by a HIGHER LAW.

Let us put the Divine Word on this Balancing Act: *"Behold, the Lord GOD shall come with a strong hand, And His arm shall rule for Him; Behold, His reward is with Him, And His work before Him. He will feed His flock like a shepherd; He will gather the lambs with His arm, And carry them in His bosom, And gently lead those who are with young. Who has measured the waters in the hollow of His hand, Measured heaven with a span And calculated the dust of the earth in a measure? Weighed the mountains in scales And the hills in a balance? Who has directed the Spirit of the LORD, Or as His counselor has taught Him? With whom did He take counsel, and who instructed Him, And taught Him in the path of justice? Who taught Him knowledge, And showed Him the way of understanding? Behold, the nations are as a drop in a bucket, And are counted as the small dust on the scales; Look, He lifts up the isles as a very little thing."* Isaiah 40:10-15.

How can we make this Balancing Act work in our favor as Believers without becoming categorized as a drop in the bucket? First, to become the Divine Bucket instead of a drop in it or a teardrop, we must become AWARE of our actions, thoughts, behaviors, tendencies, biases, words, desires, beliefs, and mental chatter, determining whether it is good or bad, right or wrong, just or unjust, and so on. Secondly, we must understand our WHY or the ROOT of whatever, whenever, however, wherever, and with whomever. Thirdly, we must make the CHANGE from our ways to God's Divine Way.

Whether the Balancing Act takes place through our occupations, hobbies, parenthood, relationships, or people skills, we can use our Divine Creativity to bring love, joy, beauty, inspiration, and innovation to the Heaven on Earth Experience of those we encounter. Although we cannot please or save everyone, the Fruits of the Spirit and Christlike Character pack a powerful punch on behalf of the Kingdom, even if we do not understand or agree with how God operates or trains them or us.

How do we know if we are on the right track with benevolence, *As It Pleases God*? Although we are all different and have our own unique stories to tell based on our backgrounds, culture, conditioning, traumas, hangups, weaknesses, and so on, He still weighs the HEART POSTURE of mankind. What does this mean in layman's terms? Amid our righteousness or wrongness, He will take note of what we are offering characteristically. Here is a list of charactorial examples about understanding how the Proof Is In The Pudding, but not limited to such:

- ☐ Are you offering kindness or unkindness?
- ☐ Are you offering compassion or hateful resentment?
- ☐ Are you offering goodwill or animosity?
- ☐ Are you offering friendliness or unfriendliness?
- ☐ Are you approachable or repulsive?
- ☐ Are you offering generosity or stinginess?
- ☐ Are you offering charity or selfishness?
- ☐ Are you offering sympathy or coldheartedness?
- ☐ Are you offering empathy or callousness?
- ☐ Are you offering love or hatefulness?
- ☐ Are you offering consideration or inconsideration?
- ☐ Are you offering respect or disrespectfulness?
- ☐ Are you offering tolerance or intolerance?
- ☐ Are you offering understanding or insensitivity?
- ☐ Are you offering forgiveness or unforgiveness?
- ☐ Are you offering grace or harshness?
- ☐ Are you offering mercy or disregard?
- ☐ Are you offering graciousness or indifference?
- ☐ Are you offering trust or mistrust?
- ☐ Are you offering peace or confusion?
- ☐ Are you offering likability or putridness?
- ☐ Are you offering integrity or unreliability?

What if we haphazardly choose to remain malevolent, opting not to make a willful effort to repent, forgive, or become better, stronger, and wiser, *As It Pleases God*? We have free will to do so, but it does not negate the adverse effects associated with the decision to remain complacent with this particular mindset.

Nor does having free will deface the repercussions of trying to beat the system or pushing the limit of the system set in place to save us. What system is there to beat? The System of God, to be exact. Regardless of our choices, we must remember: *"The eyes of the Lord are in every place, keeping watch on the evil and the good."* Proverbs 15:3. Hebrews 13:2 warns: *"Do not forget to entertain strangers, for by so doing some have unwittingly entertained angels."*

Please allow me to Spiritually Align what happens when we attempt to beat the Spiritual System designed to keep us balanced with a Creative Mindset. *"To whom then will you liken God? Or what likeness will you compare to Him? The workman molds an image, The goldsmith overspreads it with gold, And the silversmith casts silver chains. Whoever is too impoverished for such a contribution Chooses a tree that will not rot; He seeks for himself a skillful workman To prepare a carved image that will not totter. Have you not known? Have you not heard? Has it not been told you from the beginning? Have you not understood from the foundations of the earth? It is He who sits above the circle of the earth, And its inhabitants are like grasshoppers, Who stretches out the heavens like a curtain, And spreads them out like a tent to dwell in. He brings the princes to nothing; He makes the judges of the earth useless."* Isaiah 40:18-23.

How can we become useless in the Eye of God, especially when we have free will to engage or disengage in Kingdom Use or Creativity? The feeling of uselessness scatters the human psyche in ways that are yet to be discovered by Science. Why does the Field of Science not have the one-up on this matter? It is Spiritual!

According to the Heavenly of Heavens, no two Spiritual Assignments are precisely the same, requiring a *Spirit to Spirit* Connection with our Heavenly Father to download the Divine Details! Without Spiritual Authority to tread in this area,

Spiritual Violations are created. From my perspective, this is similar to entering a person's house without their consent while spying or taking what does not belong to them. According to the laws of the land, they have the right to stand their ground to protect themselves, and so it is in the Realm of the Spirit! Now, those who understand this Spiritual Law can and will enforce it.

In the Balancing Act, those who DO NOT know or understand Spiritual Laws, Principles, or Violations allow people, places, and things to do what it does, or they overlook them altogether. Then again, they become passive while surrendering to illegal encroachments, yokes, and bondages.

Why would this happen to us as Believers of the Most High God? We cannot enforce what we do not know or understand in the natural or Supernatural. Unfortunately, for this reason, we have become susceptible to the MISUSE of God, Spirituality, the Kingdom, the Holy Spirit, and the Blood of Jesus in our prayers, daily walk, character, thoughts, behaviors, and so on. Sadly, this misuse creates a Scarcity Mindset in those who do not know how to break it, *As It Pleases God*.

Scarcity Mindset

When asked if we have a Scarcity Mindset, most would answer 'no' to this question. However, it may not be the truth about this particular mindset because, most often, the best of us intentionally lie about it. Why would we lie? The reasons will vary from person to person, situation to situation, trauma to trauma, position to position, audition to audition, and so on. Nonetheless, I will say this: When we are driven by power, money, sex, and status, we will be amazed at what we will do to scar a city or scare a city! What does this mean? It is often centered around fear tactics of control, manipulation, and bullying.

Why would this mindset happen to us when we are sold out to the Kingdom of God and love Him with all our hearts? According to the Heavenly of Heavens, in the Balancing Act, we all will face this situation, much like catching a common cold or dealing with positive and negative situations, circumstances, or events. They all provoke the mind to heal itself, turn against itself, or get our mental wheels turning in the correct direction, transforming this mindset into one of the two:

- ☐ The-Lord-Will-Provide Mindset.
- ☐ The-Lord-Will-NOT-Provide Mindset.

Why are the two mindsets relevant in the Eye of God? One is designed to work for us when coupled with trust, faith, obedience, selflessness, and humility, *As It Pleases God.* The other is destined to work against us in due season due to fear, doubt, rebellion, callousness, selfishness, anger, revenge, unforgiveness, and unbelief to please ourselves. On the other hand, it is also used to carry out a debauched agenda with Him nowhere in the equation.

What is the importance of transforming to The-Lord-Will-Provide Mindset? We have a choice of becoming one of the three:

- ☐ We provide for ourselves. (Self-Sufficient).
- ☐ They provide for us. (Co-Dependant).
- ☐ The-Lord-Will-Provide using any means necessary. (Spirit Led).

For the record, we have free will to choose any of the above mindsets we like. Just know this: If there is no formal threat, we must question the value associated. How do we make this make sense? Simply put, the enemy DOES NOT attack a child of God unless there is hidden or unrecognized value. Nor does the enemy waste time and resources attacking those who are not a real threat. A threat to what? His agenda, whatever it may be!

Does God want us to suffer? No, He does not want anyone to suffer. Thus, He gives us the Word as a Spiritual Weapon of Warfare, the Blood of Jesus as Atonement, the Holy Spirit to guide, and the Spiritual Tools necessary to overcome whatever, whenever, wherever, however, and with whomever, building strength, wisdom, understanding, and know-how to resist the schemes of the enemy and stand firm, *As It Pleases Him*.

As Believers, we often find ourselves facing various challenges, trials, setbacks, and tribulations. Rest assured that it is easy to become discouraged or dumbfounded and wonder why we are facing such difficulties. However, it is also important to remember that the goal is to self-correct amid the lapse and follow instructions in Philippians 4:19, knowing: *"My God shall supply all your needs according to His riches in glory by Christ Jesus."*

More importantly, we must understand that there is a Spiritual Seal attached to The Lord-Will-Provide Covenant, Mindset, or place IN HIM. What is it? *"And Abraham called the name of the place, The-LORD-Will-Provide; as it is said to this day, 'In the Mount of the LORD it shall be provided.' Then the Angel of the LORD called to Abraham a second time out of heaven, and said: 'By Myself I have sworn, says the LORD, because you have done this thing, and have not withheld your son, your only son—blessing I will bless you, and multiplying I will multiply your descendants as the stars of the heaven and as the sand which is on the seashore; and your descendants shall possess the gate of their enemies. In your seed all the nations of the earth shall be blessed, because you have obeyed My voice.'"* Genesis 22:14-18

The Scarcity Mindset is characterized by a fear of not having enough, which can profoundly impact our Spirituality, faith, hopefulness, and self-honesty. Plus, it affects our walk with God and our ability to be authentic with ourselves while demanding honesty and loyalty from others.

Often enough, we associate a Scarcity Mindset with material gain, forgetting how it impacts us as a whole, fostering a sense of inadequacy, unfruitfulness, illegitimacy, and unworthiness. All of this leads to Spiritual Emptiness and distorted perceptions, which are caused by avoiding the uncomfortable truths about ourselves, our environment, others, and our choices. When we lack personal development, *As It Pleases God*, we inadvertently place a halt on our Spiritual Development or Classroom.

Why are we placed in a holding pattern? I would not classify this as a holding pattern but a cycle of déjà vu. In my opinion, it is similar to retaking the same test over and over with different characters with increasing intensities until we learn the lessons needed. Manifesting while in denial or a cycle of self-deception and self-delusion, with a reluctance to acknowledge our shortcomings, stunts growth and creates false associations.

How do we break the Scarcity Mindset, *As It Pleases God*? We must recalibrate our associations, understanding, trust, and faith in the Holy Trinity, use the Fruits of the Spirit, and behave Christlike while praying, fasting, repenting, forgiving, and meditating on the Word of God with thanksgiving. Once recalibrated, *As It Pleases Him*, Isaiah 58:11 says, *"The Lord will guide you continually, and satisfy your soul in drought, and strengthen your bones; you shall be like a watered garden, and like a spring of water, whose waters do not fail."*

What is the purpose of doing all of this, and why do we still fail? In the Kingdom of God, we associate our mindsets with fruits, behaviors, thoughts, actions, desires, lusts, words, biases, conditioning, heart posture, and character traits. If failure appears, it means there is a LESSON attached. Learn it, create a win-win, and share what we have learned, *As It Pleases Him*.

Suppose we fail to Spiritually Align with our Divine Assignment, *As It Pleases God*, or engage in Spiritual Violations? In this case, we become Spiritually Scattered from the inside out by default with a Scarcity Mindset, even if we pretend to have it all together. Really? Yes, really! Unfortunately, this is why we have a lot of player-hating taking place to knowingly or unknowingly scatter each other, especially by those secretly or openly feeling or experiencing uselessness. Is this Biblical? Absolutely! *"Scarcely shall they be planted, Scarcely shall they be sown, Scarcely shall their stock take root in the earth, When He will also blow on them, And they will wither, And the whirlwind will take them away like stubble."* Isaiah 40:24.

Having our creativity stubbed or stunted is one of the worst feelings we can experience, even if we do not talk about it much or are hiding it. Why are we not discussing this matter, especially among Believers? Most do not understand that it evokes jealousy, envy, pride, greed, coveting, and competitiveness, making us wishy-washy, pretentious, contentious, and condescending. Nor do we understand the ramifications or solutions to this matter. As a result, we overlook it or pretend it is not happening, opting to put on a show for people, engage in idolatry, or become swept away by the appeasing illusion of power, money, and sex. Here are some of the adverse effects associated with, but not limited to such:

- ☐ Corruption.
- ☐ Greed.
- ☐ Arrogance.
- ☐ Deceit.
- ☐ Exploitation.
- ☐ Addiction.

- ☐ Isolation.
- ☐ Betrayal.
- ☐ Debauchery.
- ☐ Cluelessness.
- ☐ Loneliness.
- ☐ Lack of trust.
- ☐ Loss of empathy.
- ☐ Loss of compassion.
- ☐ Loss of self-respect.
- ☐ Loss of dignity.
- ☐ Loss of integrity.
- ☐ Loss of morality.
- ☐ Loss of happiness.
- ☐ Loss of love.
- ☐ Loss of creativity.
- ☐ Lack of self-control.

To add insult to injury, we overlook the hidden yokes associated with the lust of the eyes, the lust of the flesh, and the pride of life. Why must we become aware of these hidden yokes as Believers? Everything that blocks the Creative Mindset will fall under one or more of these three categories, causing us to get a SPIRITUAL SIDE-EYE from our Heavenly Father. So, in the Balancing Act, we must:

- ☐ Diligently Document.
- ☐ Gain Divine Knowledge, Wisdom, and Understanding.
- ☐ Understand what is in the pudding mixture.
- ☐ Overcome the Scarcity Mindset.

In doing so, there is no limit to what we can achieve, especially when adding God into the equation of all things, *As It Pleases Him.*

Chapter 3

Spiritual Side-Eye

Have you ever received a Spiritual Side-Eye from God Almighty? Do you know what it feels like to get one? Does God feel let down when you fail to show kindness and compassion to others? Do you even care? Well, in this chapter, we are going to get down to the nitty-gritty about the shady matters of the heart that put a damper on your Creative Mindset, preventing you from becoming the cream of the crop or the crème de la crème.

The bottom line is that how God sees you matters! How you see yourself matters even more! How men see you through His Divine Eyes is like icing on the cake. So, it is not wise to get a Spiritual Side-Eye from Him. Know this: *"Behold, the eye of the Lord is on those who fear Him, On those who hope in His mercy."* Psalm 33:18. He says to us: *"I will instruct you and teach you in the way you should go; I will guide you with My eye."* Psalm 32:8.

Why should we avoid getting a Side-Eye from God when operating with free will? Scripturally, *"For we are His workmanship, created in Christ Jesus for good works, which God prepared beforehand that we should walk in them."* Ephesians 2:10. And, free will does not supersede Divine Will; it only prolongs the process until we concede.

On the contrary, if we are receiving a Spiritual Side-Eye, rest assured that we are also getting one from the average man who may or may not have the guts to tell us that our character sucks. Then again, they may not want to hurt our feelings. Here is the deal regarding getting an open or hidden side-eye: *"The rod and rebuke give wisdom, but a child left to himself brings shame to his mother."* Proverbs 29:15. If we are surrounded by shame or shamefulness, we must check our charactorial traits.

Why must we do a charactorial check-up? Proverbs 11:3 tells us that: *"The integrity of the upright will guide them, but the perversity of the unfaithful will destroy them."* Simply put, it is an indication that our Spiritual Compass is keeled in some way, our conscience is becoming desensitized, or our senses and discernment faculties have become thwarted.

What is a Spiritual Side-Eye? It is a look that God gives us, especially when we know better and choose not to do better. Or when we have Spiritual Home Training and choose not to use it, especially among those who do not know any better.

In my opinion, getting a side-eye is similar to receiving a particular look from our parents when misbehaving. We know what this means, even if they are incredibly cordial in their approach. Here are a few examples of the side-eye analogy we can get from people or a few that we are grappling with ourselves, but not limited to such:

- ☐ Being given a dubious glance.
- ☐ Receiving a skeptical look.
- ☐ Getting the evil eye.
- ☐ Facing a critical stare.
- ☐ Being the recipient of a disapproving gaze.
- ☐ Getting a judgmental look.
- ☐ Being met with a suspicious expression.
- ☐ Receiving a look of reproach.
- ☐ Getting a disapproving frown.
- ☐ Being given a withering stare.
- ☐ Facing a scathing look.
- ☐ Getting a look of disdain.
- ☐ Being met with a contemptuous expression.

- ☐ Receiving a look of disappointment.
- ☐ Getting an unimpressed stare.
- ☐ Being given a dismissive glance.
- ☐ Facing a disapproving glare.
- ☐ Getting a glare of disgust.
- ☐ Being met with a look of disbelief.
- ☐ Receiving a look of contempt.

The sidebar actions, thoughts, behaviors, and innuendos that provoke a Spiritual Side-Eye are not something we want to take lightly. Proverbs 28:22 says, "*A man with an evil eye hastens after riches, And does not consider that poverty will come upon him.*" Most would think this scripture deals with our cash flow, but it is more geared toward charactorial poverty within the Mind, Body, Soul, and Spirit. Please allow me to Spiritually Align: "*But if your eye is bad, your whole body will be full of darkness. If therefore the light that is in you is darkness, how great is that darkness!*" Matthew 6:23.

Can we really see the Spiritual Side-Eye? Absolutely! Yet, it is often ignored or downplayed due to the lack of understanding, use, or relevancy. Here is the deal: It is an inaudible experience that can be seen or felt within the conscience with a pictorial glimpse of something that we can relate to. For example, in our mind's eye, we would hear our mom's voice saying, 'You know better than that.' Then, a picture of an event will follow, describing the exact moment we suffered a consequence of that particular statement. Here are a few things that happen when we are operating in Spiritual Error, but not limited to such:

- ☐ We tend to hurt others' feelings.
- ☐ We may lose our friends and loved ones.
- ☐ We may become lonely and isolated.
- ☐ We will tend to use or abuse people.

- ☐ We may develop a negative reputation.
- ☐ We may operate with a reckless demeanor.
- ☐ We may miss out on opportunities to help others.
- ☐ We may become less empathetic towards others.
- ☐ We may struggle with trust issues.
- ☐ We may experience guilt and regret.
- ☐ We may struggle with our self-esteem.
- ☐ We may equate our worth with material gain or status.
- ☐ We may become more stressed and anxious.
- ☐ We may struggle with adverse addictions.
- ☐ We may struggle with prioritizing relationships.
- ☐ We may struggle with intimacy.
- ☐ We may struggle with forgiveness.
- ☐ We may struggle with apologizing.
- ☐ We may operate with a thwarted perspective.
- ☐ We may struggle with personal growth.
- ☐ We may become resistant to change.
- ☐ We may become less resilient as we struggle.
- ☐ We may feel unable to cope with difficult situations.
- ☐ We may freak out frequently.
- ☐ We may struggle with creativity.
- ☐ We may lack focus.
- ☐ We may become more closed-minded.
- ☐ We may be less receptive to new ideas.
- ☐ We may become more self-destructive.
- ☐ We may lack prioritization skills.
- ☐ We may shift responsibility or the blame to others.
- ☐ We may struggle with finding meaning and purpose.

If we fail to use our Spiritual Home Training among Believers and non-believers alike, we risk facing the consequences of our actions, even if we pretend we are doing what we do for the Kingdom of God. Why do we have to account for failing to use our Spiritual Home Training? It takes the same amount of energy or less to ask for wisdom as it would to do what we so desire to do without it.

Simply put, in the Eye of God, it takes more energy to pursue without Him than it would with Him at the forefront, with fewer consequences, more creativity, and less shame. Is God really the missing link to our creativity? Absolutely! It is wrapped in the one thing we all think we have. What is that? WISDOM. We all think we are rightfully wise in our own eyes without God, not realizing through whom wisdom comes. When our approach to wisdom is encroached upon, Shamefulness will follow unless we ask God for it, *As It Pleases Him*. James 1:5 says, *"If any of you lacks wisdom, let him ask of God, who gives to all liberally and without reproach, and it will be given to him."*

Shamefulness

The hidden elements of Shamefulness have been swept under the rug for too long. Now is the time to expose this powerful and complex emotion that can have a significant impact on us, our lives, and those around us.

Shamefulness is often described as an underlying painful feeling of humiliation or distress caused by the consciousness of wrongfulness or when engaging in dubious or foolish behavior. While shame is a natural emotion from our conscience, it is also a hidden alert or red flag that has been overlooked and pushed aside for far too long. It is time to shine a light on the hidden aspects of Shamefulness and address them openly and honestly, *As It Pleases God*.

Shamefulness can manifest itself in various forms, such as but not limited to such:

- ☐ Body Shame.
- ☐ Cultural Shame.
- ☐ Societal Shame.

- ☐ Financial Shame.
- ☐ Sexuality Shame.
- ☐ Status Shame.
- ☐ Family Dynamics Shame.
- ☐ Academic Shame.
- ☐ Health Disabilities Shame.
- ☐ Mental Health Shame.
- ☐ Performance Shame.
- ☐ Relationship Shame.
- ☐ Shame about one's past.
- ☐ Appearance Shame.
- ☐ Capabilities Shame.
- ☐ Mistakes Shame.
- ☐ Belief's Shaming.
- ☐ Dream Shaming.
- ☐ Desire Shaming.
- ☐ Goal Shaming.

These examples illustrate the diverse ways in which shame can manifest in our daily lives and can lead to feelings of unworthiness and self-doubt. Unfortunately, no one is immune to its effects, regardless of whether we are on the giving or receiving end. However, it is equally significant to understand that shame DOES NOT define our worthiness, astuteness, or capabilities in the Eye of God.

By acknowledging the pervasive nature of shame, we can start to unravel its complex web of triggering deceit and work toward healing and acceptance, *As It Pleases God*. Why must we work through shame? We are all here for a reason, and if we allow Shamefulness to camouflage our reason for being, we have some serious work to do from the inside out.

Why is shame associated with our character? Although no one is exempt from experiencing shame, our actions speak volumes about who we are in public and behind closed doors.

Just keep in mind that feeling shame and being put to shame in the Kingdom are two different things. How so? In the Eye of God, shame is attached to negative character traits more so than positive ones. *"For the Scripture says, 'Whoever believes on Him will not be put to shame.'"* Romans 10:11.

How can we, as Believers, understand the difference between Shamefulness and being put to shame? The differences are linked to mankind's mindset and heart posture. For example, when we are put to shame, it is most often hidden under anger, fear, pride, hatefulness, rudeness, resentfulness, untrustworthiness, putridness, unforgiveness, greed, ungratefulness, and the lack of positive creativity.

On the other hand, feeling ashamed is only temporary and is based upon our perceptions of whatever or whomever. Clearly, this does not mean that God will not use it for our good, but we are required to understand, learn, or grow. For this reason, whenever shame appears, we must look for a win-win or a positive reversal. Isaiah 54:4 wants you to develop this mindset to prevent stunted creativity by saying, *"Do not fear, for you will not be ashamed; neither be disgraced, for you will not be put to shame; for you will forget the shame of your youth, and will not remember the reproach of your widowhood anymore."*

Why is the stunting of our creativity associated with being put to shame? Instead of using our creativity positively, *As It Pleases God*, it is used as PLOTTING and SCHEMING, which nullifies the Creative Mindset to give way to a debaucherous one. Even if we pretend to be Creative Geniuses when leaving a putrified trail of rotten fruits, when being put to shame consistently in public and private, or when finding ourselves falling like dominoes, it leaves room for questioning or correction. What if we are okay with this happening to us? It means that our moral compass is keeled or our conscience has become desensitized. When getting to this point, serious Spiritual Intervention must occur to deyoke the psyche, similar to Saul's conversion to Paul's experience on the road to Damascus in Acts 9.

In the Kingdom, God will use anyone or anything to accomplish His Divine Purpose. Still, chastisement comes with the territory, especially when virtue is being developed within and through us. For this reason, we have the Word of God as a reference and the Fruits of the Spirit to guide us in the Spirit of Righteousness. Now, if we choose not to use them, we cannot lay the blame elsewhere. Proverbs 3:11-12 says, *"My son, do not despise the chastening of the Lord, nor detest His correction; for whom the Lord loves He corrects, just as a father the son in whom he delights."*

Spiritual Levels

Amid corrective measures, we must take into account the Spiritual Level that we are dealing with. What does this mean in layman's terms? There are LEVELS involved in how God sees us from a Divine Perspective and how we use the Creative Mindset designed to PLEASE Him. If we make a conscious decision to irresponsibly use His STUFF to conduct debauchery or to please ourselves and others without Him, we can lose a few notches off our belts or get demoted in the Realm of the Spirit. Really? Yes, really!

Spiritual Demotion is nothing one would ever want to endure because it comes with a tormenting Spirit similar to the one that tormented King Saul in 1 Samuel 16. Can this really happen to us? Absolutely. It happens all the time; we just do not share our true stories about the emptiness left behind due to rebellion, disobedience, ungratefulness, or waywardness. The truth is that no one, and I mean no one, is exempt from this state of being. However, it is not a matter of if; it is a matter of WHEN. When we are faced with being tormented by the weight of the world on our shoulders, we must know what to do and why we are doing so, similar to the

Garden of Gethsemane Experience in Matthew 26:36-46 with Jesus.

Jesus was not exempt from being overwhelmed with sorrow, saying, *"O My Father, if it is possible, let this cup pass from Me; nevertheless, not as I will, but as You will."* When dealing with a Creative Mindset, As It Pleases God, we will pass through this same experience or test where, in the moment of dire need, everyone falls asleep on us. Thus, we must recognize this state for what it is without whitewashing or sugarcoating it.

Well then, what do we do? There is no right or wrong answer here, but Colossians 3:23-24 leaves us a BIG SECRET that is no longer a secret now. *"And whatever you do, do it heartily, as to the Lord and not to men, knowing that from the Lord you will receive the reward of the inheritance; for you serve the Lord Christ."* *"Therefore, whether you eat or drink, or whatever you do, do all to the glory of God."* 1 Corinthians 10:31.

Why is there no definitive answer when feeling overwhelmed? We do not know what He is using to train, test, perfect, provoke, purify, or chasten unless the Holy Spirit advises or gives discernment. But if we do it or go through it, gleaning the lesson according to His Divine Will, we can leverage or place a Spiritual Demand on Romans 8:28. *"And we know that all things work together for good to those who love God, to those who are the called according to His purpose."*

Conversely, if we are out of Divine Purpose and selfishly pleasing ourselves, it becomes quite challenging to place a Spiritual Demand in places where we exclude God. Unfortunately, this leads to a lot of unanswered prayers and praying amiss. What does this mean? Most often, we are pimping God for our selfish wants, needs, and desires without considering His wants, needs, and desires first. Matthew 6:33 clearly says, *"Seek first the kingdom of God and His righteousness, and all these things shall be added to you."* And what do we do? We seek ourselves first, and then, we have the nerve to lie about our course of approach or actions while continuing to capitalize on Him without giving a rat's tail about our reason for being or our Predestined Blueprint.

Before ending this chapter, with or without a Spiritual Side-Eye, know this: 2 Corinthians 4:8-9 says, *"We are hard-pressed on every side, yet not crushed; we are perplexed, but not in despair; persecuted, but not forsaken; struck down, but not destroyed."* And then, with clean hands and pure heart: *"Cast your burden on the Lord, And He shall sustain you; He shall never permit the righteous to be moved."* Psalm 55:22.

Chapter 4

Hidden Hustle

The Hidden Hustle of the Kingdom is on high alert with a Clarion Call from the Heavenly of Heavens for those who are willing to break free from the constraints of fear, doubt, anger, resistance, rebellion, and complacency. From the Ancient Voices of our Forefathers, this is a call to action for individuals to step out in faith and pursue God's will for their lives, even when it seems daunting, unconventional, misunderstood, raunchy, confusing, or intimidating.

Greatness is never packaged pristinely at first sight. It is presented as a diamond in the rough, which needs a little elbow grease and purifying to bring forth what is already within! Then again, God may present us with a seed in need of time, nurturing, and love. Who knows the Mind of God, right? Well, in this chapter, we will learn more about His Divine Perspective, giving us a glimpse into His Heavenly Mindset, preparing us for what is next, even if our next is not preparing for us.

In today's fast-paced, ruthless, and competitive world, the idea of hustling is often associated with ambition, drive, hard work, sucker-punching, and player-hating. However, there is a different kind of hustle that is not often talked about...the Hidden Hustle of the Kingdom. This hustle is not about personal gain or success in the traditional sense. Instead, it is about going outside of your comfort zone to do what most only dream about doing, *As It Pleases God.*

In this Spiritual Pursuant process of the Hidden Hustle, *As It Pleases God*, it requires a willingness to embrace discomfort, uncertainty, chaos, and even opposition. In addition, we must be open to taking risks, making sacrifices, enduring hardships, and undergoing intense Spiritual Training for the sake of fulfilling God's Divine Purpose. Why must we go through all of this? The enemy will stop at nothing to take us down, and if we are unprepared, they will set us up for the ultimate takedown. For this reason, the Hidden Hustle demands perseverance, resilience, and unwavering faith in the face of adversity, taking the sting out of the hustle mentality and getting a grip on our emotions.

Are we not supposed to hustle and make our dreams a reality? Of course. According to the Heavenly of Heavens, we must do our due diligence, Spiritually Tilling the GIFT of our own ground. Ecclesiastes 3:13 says, *"And also that every man should eat and drink and enjoy the good of all his labor—it is the gift of God."* In addition, we must also know: *"He who tills his land will have plenty of bread, But he who follows frivolity will have poverty enough!"* Proverbs 28:19.

The question remains in the Hidden Hustle from within: Is it your dream or the Divine Will of God? Are you Spiritually Tilling your own ground for yourself or the Kingdom? Wait, wait, wait...here is another question, 'Is everything about you, or is it about the Will of God in your life?' Do you know about your Predestined Blueprint, or do you know about someone else's business better than your own? Need I ask more?

Well, please allow me to say more: 1 Thessalonians 4:11-12 says, *"That you also aspire to lead a quiet life, to mind your own business, and to work with your own hands, as we commanded you, that you may walk properly toward those who are outside, and that you may lack nothing."* In lacking nothing from the Heavenly of Heavens, we must understand this is NOT about seeking recognition or accolades from people, places, things, or the world; it is about

PLEASING God and being about our Father's Business. Now, if the psyche is seeking more than this, then we have work to do.

Why must we work on ourselves as Believers who want more out of life? Wanting more and getting more are like apples and oranges in the Eye of God. This selfless pursuant hustle is guided by love, compassion, and a desire to bring about positive change for the Greater Good.

Here is the deal: God does not mind us having dreams or desires. Is it not He who placed them there in the first place? Is it not He who granted the Creative Mindset for all to glean? Even Proverbs 21:5 says, *"The plans of the diligent lead surely to plenty, but those of everyone who is hasty, surely to poverty."* It is the most common and profound TEST known to man, yet we fail it time and time again. What TEST do we fail the most? The Divine Order test!

In the Book of Genesis, God established Divine Order for us to emulate. Yet, we see it as a nursery rhyme that we debate over who is right or wrong instead of using it as a Blueprinted Sample of His Divine Expectations. Do we think for a minute that He shared the first through the seventh day for His sake? Absolutely not! It is for our sake and our Heaven on Earth Experiences, especially when embarking upon unfamiliar territory, facing unexpected challenges, and encountering resistance where we have Divine Dominion.

Listen, the Book of Genesis shares how to establish Divine Order on how to walk the walk and talk the talk, *As It Pleases Him*, while putting all things, including our words, prophecies, and bloodlines, into their respective places. How so? Suppose we were to create a Biblical Reference of ourselves; what would it say? Blasphemy, right? Wrong. Please allow me to paint a picturesque view of a way to approach our Predestined Blueprint or reason for being, *As It Pleases God*:

- ☐ In the **Beginning** of our Heaven on Earth Experience, what would our Divine Blueprint say? (What is the Divine Mission, Goal, or Purpose?)

- ☐ On the **Second Day**, after the evening and the morning, what would our Divine Blueprint have us do? (Document the instructions, details, or absolutes).

- ☐ On the **Third Day**, after the evening and the morning, what would our Divine Blueprint have us do? (Document the instructions, details, or absolutes).

- ☐ On the **Fourth Day**, after the evening and the morning, what would our Divine Blueprint have us do? (Document the instructions, details, or absolutes).

- ☐ On the **Fifth Day**, after the evening and the morning, what would our Divine Blueprint have us do? (Document the instructions, details, or absolutes).

- ☐ On the **Sixth Day**, after the evening and the morning, what would our Divine Blueprint have us do? (Document the instructions, details, or absolutes).

- ☐ On the **Seventh Day**, after the evening and the morning, we must allow our Divine Blueprint to rest, rejuvenate, and relish the GOODNESS of the Lord, *As It Pleases Him.*

Do we think for a minute that our Heavenly Father would not honor this Divine Agreement when drawing strength from our faith, *As It Pleases Him*? He would...He will...and He does! Really? Yes, really! *"And let the beauty of the Lord our God be upon us, And establish the work of our hands for us; Yes, establish the work of our hands."* Psalm 90:17. When adding God, *Spirit to Spirit*, into the equation of all things, *As It Pleases Him*, His Divine Assurance will be with us every step of the way. Even amid those who do not understand or support our Divine Calling, Mission, Blueprint, or Passion, He will make a way for us with a Spiritual Negev (Underground Resources of Divine Provisions).

As a matter of fact, you are reading what He will do and what He has done with the Creative Mindset that also lies within you as well. You just have to get started creating, and the creativity will begin to flow. The more you flow in your creativity, *As It Pleases God*, the more it becomes Divine Creativity instead of regular or average creativity. Is there a difference? Absolutely.

In the same way that there is a difference between hot, cold, lukewarm, and frozen water, the same applies to creativity. Know this: *"Whatever your hand finds to do, do it with your might; for there is no work or device or knowledge or wisdom in the grave where you are going."* Ecclesiastes 9:10. Is this not a little insensitive? Perhaps, but dying a slow death from the inside out due to the lack of pursuing our reason for being is more insensitive, especially if I do not mention it.

According to the Ancient of Days, the Creative Mindset is an essential part of our human nature, driving us to explore new ideas and push beyond our self-imposed limitations to create something unique, strategic, and meaningful to our passions, likes, desires, or Hidden Hustle from within. It is through this mindset that we are able to imagine, form, and manifest newness, whether it be in the form of art, music, writing, science, technology, on the mission field, or any other field of our endeavors. It is also how we engage in transcending boundaries and empowering others from all walks of life to make an impacting and positive difference in their neck of the woods and beyond.

Even if we feel clueless right now, please know that what we need, we already possess. How do I know? Exodus 31:3 says, *"And I have filled him with the Spirit of God, in wisdom, in understanding, in knowledge, and in all manner of workmanship."* If we quote this back to God with courageous obedience and unwavering faith, do we think for a minute that He would ignore us? Absolutely not, especially when we do not ignore Him! Here is how to remind Him when in our *Spirit to Spirit* Communion time:

- ☐ My Father, You have filled me with the Holy Spirit.
- ☐ You have already given me the wisdom to do _____.
- ☐ Lord, unveil the understanding that I need for _____.
- ☐ Lord, grant me the know-how and how-to of _____.
- ☐ I am Your workmanship for my Predestined Blueprint.
- ☐ I cover all my endeavors with the Blood of Jesus.
- ☐ I give thanks for all that You do for and through me. Amen, Amen, and Amen.

When we tap into this Creative Mindset or unleash our potential, *As It Pleases God*, we open ourselves up to a world of infinite possibilities, especially when our fruits and character are up to par. Can anyone really do this? Absolutely! When we permit ourselves or agree to explore our ideas, thoughts, desires, and passions, or express ourselves in new and unique ways, we begin to tap into the Creative Portals from within.

Here is the deal on the Hidden Hustle: When tapping in, *As It Pleases God*, we must gather, document, analyze thoroughly, seek His Divine Guidance, and make a decision based on relevant findings. What if we get it wrong? Then, my question would be, 'What if we get it right?

All in all, in building a Creative Mindset, God is looking for teachability, learnability, documentation, roadmaps, and execution. I cannot tell you how many times I got it wrong, nor can I tell you how many times I got it right. But I will say this: Here we are NOW for a time such as this. Plus, the Divine Wisdom, along with the Divine Insights that I gleaned from the Heavenly of Heavens, will outlive me and help others to the end of time.

Is this End Time impact not a little arrogant here? Absolutely not! It is SELFLESSNESS operating to bring forth the crème de la crème. What does this mean? If you want to pay the price I paid for this information, then have at it! I intentionally laid the GROUNDWORK for you to understand where we are missing the mark in the Eye of God. With this Silver Plattered Information, *As It Pleases Him*, there is no need to recreate the wheel here. The goal is to make it better, stronger, and more resilient, allowing the cream of the crop to rise to the top in due season.

So, if you are ready to go a little deeper into this matter and are WILLING to trust God while boldly pursuing His Divine Will for your life, no matter where it may lead, then let us go as the Deep Calleth To The Deep!

Deep Calleth To The Deep

When life calls your name, are you equipped to answer? When your Predestined Blueprint demands your attention, are you equipped to put in the work? When your Spiritual Gifts are ready to be shared among your brethren, are your people skills palatable? When the Deep Calleth To The Deep, can you recognize the Voice from within? These are the questions that are on the table for those who may have lost their way but cannot tell anyone what they are experiencing. However, all hope is not lost because this is a part of the Spiritual Journey most people do not talk about. And since I am not like most people, let us get the ball rolling on this matter.

Visualizing our progress through documentation, roadmaps, or mind maps can be a game-changer in achieving mutually beneficial outcomes, even amidst errors, mistakes, blockages, setbacks, and challenges. Regardless of whether we get it right or wrong, no one is exempt from gleaning the Spiritual Benefits associated with following Divine Order according to their Predestined Blueprint. Nevertheless, it is our responsibility to engage *Spirit to Spirit* with our Heavenly Father to gain Divine Insight. 2 Thessalonians 3:10-12 says, *"For even when we were with you, we commanded you this: If anyone will not work, neither shall he eat. For we hear that there are some who walk among you in a disorderly manner, not working at all, but are busybodies. Now those who are such we command and exhort through our Lord Jesus Christ that they work in quietness and eat their own bread."*

Would Divine Insight really make a big difference in our lives as Believers, making our own bread edible? Absolutely! Divine Insight works hand in hand with Divine Discernment. Most would think they are the same, but they are not. In the Eye of God, they are Spiritual Siblings in the Realm of the Spirit, watching out for each other. How so? Divine Insight sees into things through our Spiritual Lenses for absolutes based on tangible or intangible evidence. In comparison, Divine Discernment picks up potentialities, abstracts, or manifestations without having the facts or absolutes and with the ability to change at the drop of a dime.

If we confuse the two, it is possible to make a permanent decision over a temporary circumstance. For example, if someone yells in the store, we can discern that there is a problem nearby. Meanwhile, two aisles over, we gained insight into someone who stubbed their toe on a shopping cart because they were limping. Although this example is in the natural, the same applies to the Spiritual. More importantly, they contain Spiritual Rules, Laws, and Principles we all must heed to prevent Spiritual Abuse, similar to what occurred with Adam and Eve in the Book of Genesis.

Here is one of the elements of the Hidden Hustle that we miss time and time again: *"Therefore, brethren, desire earnestly to prophesy, and do not forbid to speak with tongues. Let all things be done decently and in order."* 1 Corinthians 14:39-40. What does this scripture have to do with anything, especially the Book of Genesis? Or better yet, how do we make this make sense? From Genesis to Revelation (from the Beginning to the End), we are all prophets of our own lives once Divine Order is established, *As It Pleases God.* If we delegate this task to someone else, then we cannot lay the blame elsewhere for lacking discernment in this area. While there are some things we can delegate, unfortunately, this is not one of them.

Why can we NOT delegate Divine Creativity when developing a Creative Mindset? First, if we delegate this area, we will always end up insecure, lacking authenticity, or looking like boo-boo the fool. Besides, who wants to become a creative fool of folly? For the record, I am not calling anyone names here; I am only establishing a classification in the Eye of God. Proverbs 1:7 says, *"The fear of the Lord is the beginning of knowledge, but fools despise wisdom and instruction."*

Secondly, we can always get help in this area...still, we never want to skip out on the classroom because there are certain things that only we can learn on our Spiritual Journey. If we opt not to learn, it places us in a cycle of déjà vu, taking two steps forward and three steps back. Proverbs 12:15 says, *"The way of a fool is right in his own eyes, but he who heeds counsel is wise."*

Thirdly, we must learn how to follow instructions, period. If we delegate instructions or corrective measures designed for us, we cannot develop our Spiritual Instincts or calibrate our Spiritual Compass. Proverbs 15:5 says, *"A fool despises his father's instruction, but he who receives correction is prudent."* Entrusting someone with the responsibility of the Creative Forces guarding our Creative Mindset is like having someone eat the food that is designed to nourish us. The bottom line is that Creative Delegation is a NO-GO in the Kingdom!

What is the big deal about Creative Delegation? In the Eye of God, it is the deal-breaker between mediocrity and GREATNESS. In Divine Order or when overcoming, Divine Creativity has its own Spiritual Language or Tongue hidden within it that no one can decode outside of the Holy Trinity and the one who possesses it. So, if our language is not languaging or adding up, we are tapped into the wrong SOURCE. Revelation 12:11 says, *"And they overcame him by the blood of the Lamb and by the word of their testimony, and they did not love their lives to the death."*

Still, when things are not copasetic from within, and the math is not mathing or multiplying as it should, we may find ourselves doing nothing, saying nothing, overreacting, acting out, or overlooking God altogether. Why must we add God to the equation? The Book of Genesis says several times to be fruitful and multiply, so it is only wise to add Him, the Giver of multiplication, adding, subtracting, and dividing. If we subtract the Giver of life from our equational efforts, the zero becomes inevitable. How so? For example, we walk around as if we created the Word of God ourselves with zero order or zero self-control in our thoughts, words, emotions, desires, actions, reactions, or whatever.

Plus, we go from day to day without a Blueprinted Plan or Divine Instructions from the Heavenly of Heavens, and think we have it going on. Sadly, in the Eye of God, this overlooked omission allows our mouths to write checks that we cannot cash here on Earth or in the Kingdom of Heaven. What does this mean? We have zero Spiritual Power in the Eye of God.

Even if we have earthly power, money, or sexing our way through life. It does not do us a bit of good when we are in a Spiritual Battle when trying to break yokes, when we are bodaciously soul-tied, or when under a Spiritual Attack. Thus, when needing things that power, money, and sex cannot buy, we are required to gear up, *As It Pleases God*. Plus, we should never allow ourselves to get to this point or become desperate before developing a *Spirit to Spirit* Relationship with our Heavenly Father.

Why must we go through hoops and gear up as Believers, especially with the things we cannot see physically? Please allow me to answer this question with a scripture. 1 Corinthians 14:36-38 says, *"Or did the word of God come originally from you? Or was it you only that it reached? If anyone thinks himself to be a prophet or spiritual, let him acknowledge that the things which I write to you are the commandments of the Lord. But if anyone is ignorant, let him be ignorant."*

To be clear, I am not calling anyone ignorant here. I am only drawing a parallel to how we fail our Divine Tests that stifle our Spiritual Credibility, Creativity, Reliability, and Authenticity, preventing our tongues from becoming the pen of a ready writer, *As It Pleases God*. But I will say this: We should never discount the things we cannot see as they relate to God.

Why should we not discount the unseen as Believers? Frankly, this is how we become deceived. How so? Let me ask a question: 'Can you see your thoughts, words, mind, psyche, conscience, senses, or Spirit? Better yet, can you see faith, trust, hope, and integrity? Can you see the oxygen you are breathing right now? Can you see the atoms and molecules holding you together? Although you can see the results or manifestations of them all, the state of origin is what makes your reality what it is.

Everything that God uses to connect with us *Spirit to Spirit*, and what binds us to our Heaven on Earth Experiences, is unseen. By far, this makes the unseen more potent than the seen. Without the unseen, there is no seen! Is this Biblical? 2 Corinthians 4:18 says, *"While we do not look at the things which are seen, but at the things which are not seen. For the things which are seen are* temporary, but the things which are not seen are eternal." "Now faith is the substance of things hoped for, the evidence of things not seen." Hebrews 11:1.

Raising Questions

In reality, when our mouths are wide open with zero order or documentation *Spirit to Spirit*, questions are being raised in the Realm of the Spirit. Why are questions being raised about us? In order for the Holy Spirit to speak on our behalf, questions must be raised in the Realm of the Spirit to convey the information and answers to us. Really? Yes, really!

When operating in a *Spirit to Spirit* Relationship, *As It Pleases God*, and when maximizing our Creative Mindset, know this: First, *"The Helper, the Holy Spirit, whom the Father will send in My name, He will teach you all things, and bring to your remembrance all things that I said to you."* John 14:26. Secondly, *"However, when He, the Spirit of truth, has come, He will guide you into all truth; for He will not speak on His own authority, but whatever He hears He will speak; and He will tell you things to come."* John 16:13. Thirdly, *"Likewise the Spirit also helps in our weaknesses. For we do not know what we should pray for as we ought, but the Spirit Himself makes intercession for us with groanings which cannot be uttered."* Romans 8:26.

What if we are clueless when speaking? When we are in Purpose on purpose, the information will flow. Then again, when we are out of purpose in a typical setting, having nothing to do with Kingdom Business, we may run into a struggle, letting us know that that is not our portion or cup of tea. Thus, we should not worry or stress about it because what we need at the appropriate time, we will have. Here is what we need to know: *"But when they deliver you up, do not worry about how or what you should speak. For it will be given to you in that hour what you should speak; for it is not you who speak, but the Spirit of your Father who speaks in you."* Matthew 10:19.

We are most often too focused on the people, places, and things we can see while neglecting the unseen. Please allow me to Spiritually Align: *"Therefore we do not lose heart. Even though our outward man is perishing, yet the inward man is being renewed day by day. For our light affliction, which is but for a moment, is working for us a far more exceeding and eternal weight of glory, while we do not look at the things which are seen, but at the things which are not seen. For the things which are seen are temporary, but the things which are not seen are eternal."* 2 Corinthians 4:16-18.

How can we change the trajectory of our words, *As It Pleases God*? Before opening our mouths or uttering one word, repeat this scripture: *"My heart is overflowing with a good theme; I recite my composition concerning the King; My tongue is the pen of a ready writer."* Psalm 45:1.

Will Psalm 45:1 really work for us? Absolutely! For example, when we are connected *Spirit to Spirit* as we should, God will not reveal something about us to someone else that He has not revealed to us. Once we are truly connected, *As It Pleases Him*, He will send CONFIRMATION. Now, if we are too busy trying to achieve the title, to prophesy over the lives of others, but fail to know the Divine Blueprint for our own lives, we will miss the cues, nudges, and red flags. More importantly, if we do not have a single word or instruction documented, giving God something to work with, we can also miss His Divine Move.

The key in the Hidden Hustle is to incorporate His Divine Will first and then add our personal stuff on the back end with a selfless approach. Psalm 37:4-5 shares this with us: *"Delight yourself also in the Lord, and He shall give you the desires of your heart. Commit your way to the Lord, Trust also in Him, and He shall bring it to pass."* If we approach God selfishly without adding Him into the equation, we set ourselves up for defeat, even when we are winning.

From this point onward, God is not having it! Having what? Having us settle for the stubble of mediocrity, especially when our Creative Mindsets are already in place and on cue. The bottom line is that we have the POWER to overcome, understand, learn, and grow through Him, and *As It Pleases Him*. Here is what He wants us to know: *"Have you not known? Have you not heard? The everlasting God, the LORD, The Creator of the ends of the earth, Neither faints nor is weary. His understanding is unsearchable. He gives power to the weak, And to those who have no might He increases strength. Even the youths shall faint and be weary, And the young men shall utterly fall, But those who wait on the LORD Shall renew their strength; They shall mount up with wings like eagles, They shall run and not be weary, They shall walk and not faint."* Isaiah 40:28-31.

From the Ancient of Days, CREATIVITY is a GIFT from God, and it is something that each one of us can cultivate and develop to please ourselves or to PLEASE HIM for the GREATER GOOD. However, to embark upon Divine Purpose, we need to factor ourselves into building a Creative Mindset that PLEASES Him to unveil our Divine Blueprint, bringing us in Purpose on purpose and taking our normal edifices of creativity to a Divine Status. What does this mean? Simply put, in Earthen Vessels, we have ordinary creativity that is accessible to anyone. And then, we have Divine Creativity from the Heavenly of Heavens with real-time downloads and uploads requiring specific prerequisites and contingencies. If we do not know what they are or are not, we deceive ourselves with the maximization of our Creative Efforts.

What if we are creative, have it going on, and need no one, including God? Unfortunately, this is how we become deceived as the psyche does a number on us from the inside out while turning on ourselves without knowing it. All this tells me is that with this mindset, our Divine Creativity is limited and that we are lying to ourselves. How can I say such a thing, right? Here is what the Bible says: *"Trust in the Lord with all your heart, And lean not on your own understanding; In all your ways acknowledge Him, And He shall direct your paths."* Proverbs 3:5-6.

If we are leading ourselves, then it is fair to say that trust is not leading us and that a proper understanding of the Mind of God is not leading our lives, *As It Pleases Him*. Who am I to judge, right? No judgment is intended; I am only providing a Spiritual Parallel before moving on because John 15:5 says, *"I am the vine, you are the branches. He who abides in Me, and I in him, bears much fruit; for without Me you can do nothing."* Frankly, if our something means nothing in the Eye of God, we have work to do!

Clearly, I am not here to judge anyone's something or nothing; I am here to invoke the Creative Mindset of creating a win-win out of whatever or with whomever, leaving no stone unturned and no WILLING man behind while learning from the unwilling. How can we leave no one behind? We cannot force anyone to keep up, but we can do our due diligence in facilitating this process. Here are a few pointers or patterns that will assist, but are not limited to such:

- ☐ Share a loving demeanor with everyone.
- ☐ Be calm and patient.
- ☐ Avoid engaging in chaos and confusion.
- ☐ Communicate openly, respectfully, and transparently.
- ☐ Believe in yourself and others.
- ☐ Keep everyone involved.
- ☐ Share hopefulness with others.
- ☐ Foster a culture of inclusivity and diversity.
- ☐ Provide opportunities for growth and development.
- ☐ Encourage collaboration and teamwork.
- ☐ Recognize and appreciate contributions.
- ☐ Be kind and thankful.
- ☐ Offer support and mentorship to those who need it.
- ☐ Ensure access to necessary resources and tools.

- ☐ Create a positive and empowering environment.
- ☐ Listen to and consider diverse perspectives and ideas.
- ☐ Celebrate achievements personally and as a team.
- ☐ Establish clear goals and expectations.
- ☐ Promote a sense of belonging.
- ☐ Advocate for fairness and righteousness.
- ☐ Address any issues or concerns promptly.
- ☐ Ask for agreement and effective feedback.
- ☐ Embrace empathy and understanding.
- ☐ Build trust and respect.
- ☐ Use the Fruits of the Spirit.
- ☐ Work on behaving Christlike at all times.

Before moving on, please allow me to share this with you: "*In all things showing yourself to be a pattern of good works; in doctrine showing integrity, reverence, incorruptibility, sound speech that cannot be condemned, that one who is an opponent may be ashamed, having nothing evil to say of you.*" Titus 2:7-8. So, let us go deeper into building the Cornerstone of Greatness with what you already possess, helping you to become Authentically Creative, *As It Pleases God*.

CHAPTER 5

Authentically Creative

According to the Heavenly of Heavens, AUTHENTICITY is the key to our Creative Genius. The moment we find ourselves lying to the Creative Forces that lie within, we become Spiritually Limited to Kingdom Treasures, Wisdom, and Secrets. Why do we become limited as Believers who are sold out to the Kingdom of God? Being sold out to the Kingdom does not mean that we are trusted with the Divine Keys, nor does it mean God is approving our method of operation. It takes time to become Spiritually Trained, *As It Pleases God.*

As it says in Ecclesiastes 3:11, *"He has made everything beautiful in its time. Also, he has put eternity into man's heart, yet so that he cannot find out what God has done from the beginning to the end."* We have been given a glimpse of the beauty and creativity that lies within us, but we can never fully understand the depth of it without the Creator of it. Nevertheless, it is our responsibility to explore, use, learn, prepare, and grow authentically and sow back into the Kingdom when called upon.

For the record, if we think we can hand God whatever to our standards and likes while pretending to be someone else or putting on a show, we are sadly mistaken. In the Eye of God, as Believers or unbelievers, without working on ourselves, *As It Pleases Him*, we will become viewed as vomit. Blasphemy, right? Wrong! *"So then, because you are lukewarm, and neither cold nor hot, I will vomit you out of My mouth."* Revelation 3:16.

Although vomit is considered repulsive, think about it like this: Imagine sending your child to the store to buy meat for dinner, only to find out that they returned with a bag of rocks purchased from a random peddler on the street. Unfortunately, they did not inspect the bag before purchasing, paid the full price, and were unable to get a refund. It is a frustrating situation that could have easily been avoided if only they had taken the time to inspect the bag before making the purchase.

While it may seem like a shortcut to take the easy way out, it is essential to remember that sometimes, the extra effort is worth it in the end. By making informed decisions, we can avoid costly mistakes and ensure that we get what we paid for.

Now the question is, 'What would you do in this situation?' 'Better yet, how would you feel?' Well, this is how God feels when giving us everything we need to succeed, but we fail to use what we have in our hands due to our perceived conditions, conveniences, circumstances, or ungratefulness. So, the next time you are faced with a choice between taking a shortcut and doing things the right way, remember the bag of rocks and choose wisely.

Why is this bag of rocks analogy so crucial in developing a Creative Mindset? The goal is to leave no stone unturned to get to the Cornerstone of Greatness, *As It Pleases God*. It does not matter if anyone or no one sees value in what you have to offer; you should not circumvent your Creative or Positive Mindset for a pile of rocks, throw rocks, or lie about your idiosyncrasies. Regardless of where you are or what you are going through, it is what it is! Just keep it moving in the Spirit of Excellence, using the Fruits of the Spirit and behaving Christlike.

Why is it so essential to maintain a positive mindset as such? A negative mindset produces negative fruits, thoughts, beliefs, desires, and character. Really? Yes, really. Proverbs 26:11 tells us that: *"As a dog returns to his own vomit, so a fool repeats his folly."* In addition, Hosea 8:7 says, *"For they have sown the wind, and they shall reap the whirlwind. The stalk has no bud; it shall never produce meal. If it should produce, aliens would swallow it up."*

Status or no status, plenty of money or no money, love or no love, having plenty of friends and family members or none at all, there is nothing worse than being a talented fool in the Eye of God. Oh my...not a talented fool! Do not be shocked by this analogy, mainly when it takes the same amount of energy to become a Creative Vessel using what you already have with a Positive Mindset, the Fruits of the Spirit, and behaving Christlike.

Does it really take the same amount of energy? Absolutely! When you repeat Philippians 4:13, *"I can do all things through Christ who strengthens me,"* over everything, you invoke that energy. On the other hand, if you speak failure and defeat over yourself, you invoke that energy as well. All in all, it is a matter of choice that determines the energy you attract and the BLESSINGS you repel or overlook. Unfortunately, due to the lack of discernment, most often, our BLESSINGS are usually perceived as feeble rocks thrown aside or kicked to the curb when they are really Diamonds in the Rough.

Then again, if we trust ourselves with lies without self-correcting or repenting, how is it possible to unveil the Truths of the Kingdom without abusing it or them? As a result, behind closed doors, the psyche will begin to do a number on us as we turn on ourselves without realizing it. Whether we admit it or not, strife will permeate our lives, pride will erect strongholds, and the lack of humility will yoke us to the core while appearing right in our own eyes.

How do we break strongholds, yokes, or bondages in public, private, and before God? First, James 4:7 says,

"Therefore submit to God. Resist the devil and he will flee from you." Secondly, we must get an understanding of God's Divine Perspective, *As It Pleases Him*. Will He really help us with them? Absolutely! Isaiah 41:10 says, *"Fear not, for I am with you; Be not dismayed, for I am your God. I will strengthen you, Yes, I will help you, I will uphold you with My righteous right hand." "But seek first the kingdom of God and His righteousness, and all these things shall be added to you."* Matthew 6:33.

In Earthen Vessels, we are often tempted to feel proud, boastful, untouchable, self-sufficient, and above God. Then again, we may think that we have everything under control and DO NOT need anyone else's help. However, if we take a closer look at the world around us and through the Lens of our Heavenly Father, we will realize that we are not as powerful, self-sufficient, and creative as we thought.

Within the blink of an eye, our stories can change for the better or worse. Thus, it is always wise to remain on the positive side of the spectrum of all things, using the Fruits of the Spirit, and behave Christlike. Why? In the Eye of God, whether we use them positively or negatively, they are considered SEEDS, making us Authentically Creative or unauthentically fake.

When developing a Creative Mindset, *As It Pleases God*, we must understand that everything has an expiry date. Once our time is up on whatever, whenever, and however, we must ensure we can sustain the seeds sown in or out of season. What does this have to do with our Creative Mindset? Whether it is our time, opportunities, status, resources, or whatever, everything is finite.

Although we know there is a time and season for everything. Still, for some odd reason, we fail to prepare, *As It Pleases God*. Only to end up selfishly pleasing ourselves to the point where everything is about us and not the Kingdom of God.

We must make the most of the time and talents we have been given, but we often fail to do so. Nor do we give God the time of day to document instructions or to scrape out a timeline regarding our next move with Him at the forefront. As a matter of fact, it is crucial to ensure that the seeds we sow, whether in our personal, private, professional, or Spiritual lives, can endure beyond our timelines, pleasures, mindsets, or agendas. Simply put, we must cultivate a Creative Mindset that is Spiritually Driven, Purposeful, and Mindful of the legacy we aim to leave behind.

According to the Heavenly of Heavens, it behooves us to understand who we are from God's Divine Perspective so that our Creative Characteristics come forth, *As It Pleases Him*. Here are a few characteristics at a glance that we should work on when becoming Authentically Creative, but not limited to such:

- ☐ Humility.
- ☐ Gratitude.
- ☐ Forgiveness.
- ☐ Compassion.
- ☐ Honesty.
- ☐ Love.
- ☐ Patience.
- ☐ Kindness.
- ☐ Faithfulness.
- ☐ Integrity.
- ☐ Obedience.
- ☐ Perseverance.
- ☐ Self-Control.
- ☐ Generosity.
- ☐ Servanthood.
- ☐ Courage.
- ☐ Wisdom.
- ☐ Discernment.

- ☐ Reverence.
- ☐ Surrender.

According to the Ancient of Days, it is essential to recognize that we are all unique individuals with different wants, needs, backgrounds, and desires. Cultivating these traits takes ongoing effort and practice, but they ultimately help us form a stronger and more meaningful connection with God, *Spirit to Spirit*.

Divine Illumination

As Spiritual Beings having a human experience, this Divine Illumination is vital to leading a fulfilling and purposeful life, *As It Pleases Him*. So, when locking in on a Creative Mindset, it is worth investing the time and energy to nurture the qualities that help us obtain, maintain, and sustain this sought-after state of being with Creative Characteristics that cannot be hidden. So, *"Let your light so shine before men, that they may see your good works and glorify your Father in heaven."* Matthew 5:16.

How do we let our lights shine and become Authentically Creative? There are many ways to become illuminated, *As It Pleases God*, so it is wise to seek His Face *Spirit to Spirit* due to varying differences and Spiritual Blueprints. Nevertheless, here are a few pointers on getting the ball rolling in the correct direction, but not limited to such:

- ☐ Pray, repent, forgive, and exhibit mercy.
- ☐ Meditate regularly to connect to God, *Spirit to Spirit*.
- ☐ Cover yourself with the Blood of Jesus as Spiritual Atonement.
- ☐ Awaken your Spirit to become ONE with the Holy Spirit.

- ☐ Use the Fruits of the Spirit to build Christlike Character.
- ☐ Keep a journal, documenting your thoughts, ideas, and instructions.
- ☐ Practice gratitude in all things.
- ☐ Remain positive and respectful.
- ☐ Remain open to new opportunities or ideas, dissecting them all.
- ☐ Remain on a learning curve, developing new skills and techniques.
- ☐ Collaborate with others.
- ☐ Share relevant thoughts, ideas, and concepts to inspire yourself and others.
- ☐ Reverse negatives to positives to create a win-win with everything.
- ☐ Embrace imperfections and learn from them.
- ☐ Use your mistakes and mishaps as stepping stones.
- ☐ Use your Spiritual Gifts to serve others.
- ☐ Set clear goals and work toward them.
- ☐ Prioritize tasks and get rid of distractions.
- ☐ Use a to-do list and a not-to-do list.
- ☐ Practice self-correcting, self-mirroring, and self-analysis.

Remember that capitalizing on a Creative Mindset is a journey, not a destination. Why would a Creative Mindset be considered a journey? In the Eye of God, you must work on taking your average journey of mediocrity to a Spiritual Journey of Greatness. Is this humanly possible, especially after making a lot of mistakes? Absolutely! From my perspective, mistakes become lessons if we learn from them, *As It Pleases God.* Even if you need to build your momentum, start over, or take small, consistent steps on your Spiritual Journey, do not give up on yourself. If you follow these few steps wholeheartedly, *As It Pleases Him,* and get your natural self out of the way, there will be no limits on what you can achieve when Divinely Illuminated.

Unlocking our full potential is dreamt about by most and only utilized by a few. But of course, this will not be you, right? After reading this book, your limitations will no longer hold you back unless you permit them to do so.

What if limits form on their own? All this means is that you must find another way that fits you or your particular situation. Why must we find another way as Believers? The win-win is always hidden under something else; therefore, we cannot leave any stones unturned. If we do not extract anything else from whatever with whomever, we must grab the LESSON, period. It is in the LESSON that Divine Illumination will power our Spiritual Lighthouse or Compass.

What if we are trained not to give up? To be clear, this is not giving up on yourself; it is merely finding another way to do what needs to be done, *As It Pleases God.*

Then again, giving up your way for God's Divine Way is not as severing as it seems because it provides a guide or redirection of Divine Illumination. However, in this phase, you must muster up enough strength to get yourself out of the way, become a work-in-progress, and move forward in the Spirit of Excellence.

Getting your natural self out of the way may require you to shed the layers of hidden insecurities, unresolved traumas, self-doubt, self-induced fears, negative self-talk, and self-limiting beliefs or thoughts holding you back from pursuing your goals, dreams, true potential, or desires, *As It Pleases God.*

What can this list of things do for someone who likes being in control? In the Eye of God, it helps rewire your mindset from negative to positive, losing to winning, bad to good, immoral to moral, and unjust to just, helping you focus on your strengths and working on your weaknesses.

How does working on weaknesses help Believers when life is lifing? First, you must take one step at a time, with the Holy Trinity at the forefront to expose, train, and present your Spiritual Gifts that are waiting to be unleashed. Secondly, your weaknesses are usually where your Spiritual Gifts are hidden. So, it is never wise to forfeit your weaknesses. Really? Yes, really!

Every weakness that I had or still have is what I use to bring forth the *As It Pleases God*® Movement for a time such as this. So, before moving to Creative Characteristics, let me say this: Never despise the day of small beginnings.

Creative Characteristics

Our Creative Characteristics are not for our own benefit alone. They are meant to be shared with others for the Greater Good, *As It Pleases God*. When using them as a service to others, we demonstrate the love of God and contribute to the building of a stronger and more unified Kingdom. Whether it is through acts of service, words of wisdom, or the sharing of talents, each person can contribute to the Greater Good through the use of their Creative Characteristics and Spiritual Gifts.

What if we do not have anything to offer anyone for the Greater Good? If you are still living, breathing the breath of life, you have something to offer. The truth of the matter is that it is only selfishness that blocks you from recognizing what to give and what to withhold. Still, regardless of how it appears to the naked eye, you are giving something, even if it is negative, harmful, or indifferent. So, if you are feeling this way, you merely need to do the opposite or reverse whatever with whomever to the positive, righteous, just, and sound.

Amid all, you must: *"Commit your works to the Lord, and your thoughts will be established."* Proverbs 16:3.

When we tap into our Creative Characteristics, *As It Pleases God*, we not only express ourselves as artistically affluent but also nurture our Mind, Body, Soul, and Spirit in the process. How does this make sense, especially when dealing with the Mind, Body, Soul, and Spirit? When dealing with our Predestined Blueprint, they are all connected in the Eye of God because each person is different from the next person. All this means is that we all have a different Mindprint, Bodyprint, Soulprint, and Spiritprint, similar to having a different fingerprint, eyeprint, footprint, and tongueprint.

In all reality, we are surrounded by forces that are beyond our control, and we are only a tiny part of the big picture, especially if we are out of purpose, pleasing ourselves, and excluding God Almighty from our equational efforts. Why would this happen to us? Although we are all different, the reasons will vary from person to person, situation to situation, bias to bias, lesson to lesson, mindset to mindset, and trauma to trauma. However, our approach matters. For example: *"And whatever you do, do it heartily, as to the Lord and not to men, knowing that from the Lord you will receive the reward of the inheritance; for you serve the Lord Christ."* Colossians 3:23-24.

God is the CREATOR of all things. He is the Divine ONE who holds everything together, and He is the SOURCE of it all, even if we do not understand Him, it, them, or that. For this reason, God requires RESPECT for all. We must acknowledge that we are sinners in need of love, repentance, forgiveness, and understanding, and no one is beyond reproach.

Plus, it is our responsibility to find true peace and happiness in a relationship with Him, *Spirit to Spirit*, opening ourselves up to the fullness of Divine Love, Grace, Mercy, and Fulfillment, *As It Pleases Him*. Here are a few things that can turn us away from God, hindering our Spiritual Growth and Creative Characteristics, but not limited to such:

- ☐ Pride and arrogance.
- ☐ Love of money and material possessions.
- ☐ Lust and sexual immorality.
- ☐ Envy and jealousy.
- ☐ Anger and resentment.
- ☐ Hatred and malice.
- ☐ Unforgiveness and bitterness.
- ☐ Idolatry and worship of false gods.
- ☐ Rebellion and disobedience.
- ☐ Selfishness and self-centeredness.
- ☐ Lack of faith and trust in God.
- ☐ Hypocrisy and dishonesty.
- ☐ Addiction and substance abuse.
- ☐ Greed and exploitation.
- ☐ Laziness and sloth.
- ☐ Impatience and impulsiveness.
- ☐ Negativity and pessimism.
- ☐ Fear and anxiety.
- ☐ Doubt and unbelief.
- ☐ Ignorance and lack of knowledge.
- ☐ Competitiveness and rudeness.

Can these items really block us as Believers? Absolutely! Most often, we deny the blockages while the psyche does a number on us, turning us against ourselves and the Creative Force lying within. All of which are reflected in our thoughts, actions, reactions, beliefs, biases, and words.

When it comes to loving God and doing what is right, we must be mindful of the knowledge we possess. Without this knowledge, our actions may unintentionally cause harm to ourselves and those around us, even if our hearts are in the right place. To truly serve Him and understand His Divine

Totality, we must seek to expand our understanding of His Divine Will and Ways. Only then can we genuinely honor Him and live a life that is fulfilling and meaningful while self-correcting or self-mirroring (examining ourselves) at the drop of a dime.

To self-correct, *As It Pleases Him*, it is essential to recognize and acknowledge adverse character traits in ourselves and work towards dealing with and overcoming them. By doing so, we can become better individuals, contribute to the Kingdom positively, cultivate positive qualities, and strive towards self-improvement.

On the other hand, there may come a time when we will encounter a standstill regarding what PLEASES God. Nonetheless, when dealing with a Creative Mindset, here are a few traits that He loves, and are all derived from the use of the Fruits of the Spirit:

- ☐ Love and compassion.
- ☐ Kindness and generosity.
- ☐ Humility and meekness.
- ☐ Forgiveness and mercy.
- ☐ Honesty and integrity.
- ☐ Faithfulness and loyalty.
- ☐ Patience and perseverance.
- ☐ Gratitude and thankfulness.
- ☐ Self-control and discipline.
- ☐ Courage and bravery.
- ☐ Wisdom and discernment.
- ☐ Creativity and innovation.
- ☐ Empathy and understanding.
- ☐ Respect and dignity.
- ☐ Responsibility and accountability.
- ☐ Excellence and attention to detail.
- ☐ Open-mindedness and flexibility.
- ☐ Optimism and positivity.

- ☐ Enthusiasm and passion.
- ☐ Selflessness and sacrifice.
- ☐ Cooperation and teamwork.
- ☐ Leadership and vision.
- ☐ Empowerment and encouragement.
- ☐ Resourcefulness and problem-solving skills.
- ☐ Adaptability and resilience.
- ☐ Sense of humor and playfulness.
- ☐ Sensitivity and gentleness.
- ☐ Authenticity and genuineness.
- ☐ Graciousness and tactfulness.
- ☐ Appreciation and admiration.

Can these positive character traits really help us when dealing with a Creative Mindset? Absolutely! Having a positive Creative Mindset involves being able to think inside, outside, through, around, over, and under the box, come up with innovative ideas, and solve complex problems. On the other hand, negativity creates known and unknown blockages, provoking or feeding other yoking and debilitating traits, similar to a plague.

How do we make this make sense to ourselves, our character traits, our mindsets, and God? Having open-mindedness and flexibility can help us explore and embrace new ideas and concepts, making us Kingdomly Usable and Kingdomly Trainable. Similarly, having the courage, tenacity, and bravery to take risks and try new things can lead to breakthrough moments in creativity in the natural. But it also does so in the Spiritual Realm. How so? Unbeknown to most, this is where the Holy Spirit can work best with us, through us, and beyond us based upon elements of RESPECT and HUMILITY.

Once we develop respect and humility, *As It Pleases God*, our Creative Characteristics will go to work on our behalf, working through our conscience, senses, thoughts, people skills, and mental pictures, sparking a sought-after Creative Mindset. In addition, it will contain Isaiah 43:19 Spiritual Seal: "*Behold, I will do a new thing, now it shall spring forth; shall you not know it? I will even make a road in the wilderness and rivers in the desert.*" These powerful words have brought renewal, hope, peace, and inspiration to countless individuals, and you are no different.

The PROMISE of something new, the PROMISE of transformation, and the PROMISE of renewal have a Divine Resonance that speaks to you, *Spirit to Spirit*, especially when challenged, when in need of change, when desiring Creative Refinement, or when seeking Divine Intervention.

CHAPTER 6

Divine Paper Trail

In the Spiritual Refining Process, we often forget about the need for Creative Refinement, not realizing it is at our beck and call. Now the question is, 'Are we forgetting because it slipped our minds?' or, 'Are we forgetting because we do not understand the need for it?' Then again, I have never come in contact with a person who is praying, 'God, refine my creativity.'

The Creative Force that lies within is a real Spiritual Commodity that goes untapped by many but is desired by all mankind. Really? Yes, really. The tugging from within the human psyche is often linked to creativity, and our creativity is linked to our passion, and our passion is linked to our Predestined Blueprint. According to the Heavenly of Heavens, this is God's Divine Paper Trail for us to follow with the inscribed details of everything we need for our Heaven on Earth Experience.

How is it humanly possible to have a Divine Paper Trail from within? For this one, let us take it to scripture: "*You are our epistle written in our hearts, known and read by all men; clearly you are an epistle of Christ, ministered by us, written not with ink but by the Spirit of the living God, not on tablets of stone but on tablets of flesh, that is, of the heart.*" 2 Corinthians 3:2-3. The Divine Paper Trail is already written on the Tablet of the Heart and is connected to our MORAL COMPASS, guiding our actions, thoughts, beliefs, words, and decisions according to God's Divine Will.

On the other hand, when the Divine Paper Trail is in a dormant state (not being used), a longing or void is felt. Why would we feel a void, especially as Believers? It is our conscience or Spiritual Compass letting us know a few things, but not limited to such:

- ☐ There is more to us than what meets the eye.
- ☐ We are off track.
- ☐ Disobedience or lack of humility is present.
- ☐ Our free will has superseded God's Divine Will.
- ☐ We have overstepped our boundaries.
- ☐ There is a glitch in our character traits.
- ☐ We are not Spiritually Tilling our own ground (not tending to our own business or being about our Father's Business).

This Divine Paper Trail runs really deep within the core of our being, giving life to our Divine Passion, Mission, or Blueprint. Fortunately, this is why writers write, painters paint, musicians play music, singers sing, dancers dance, golfers golf, preachers preach, actors act, fishermen fish, and so on.

If we think for a minute that we do not possess a Divine Paper Trail within us, we are sadly mistaken. Proverbs 3:1-4 says, *"My son, do not forget my law, But let your heart keep my commands; For length of days and long life And peace they will add to you. Let not mercy and truth forsake you; Bind them around your neck, Write them on the tablet of your heart, And so find favor and high esteem In the sight of God and man."*

Our internal values aid in guiding our actions, thoughts, beliefs, words, and desires into self-pleasure or PLEASING God. What about pleasing others? Unfortunately, to please others, we must go through one of the two doorways:

- ☐ Selfishness (pleasing ourselves). Self-serving.
- ☐ Selflessness (Pleasing God). Kingdom-Serving.

What is the purpose of knowing about these two doors? Our WHY is hidden behind them. Why we do what we do is hidden behind one of the two doors. Why we are a people pleaser is hidden behind one of the two doors. Why we are not following the Divine Paper Trail is hidden behind one of the two doors. So, you see...the WHY is always connected to whatever trail we are on. Thus, if we omit the WHY, we can get lost in the shuffle of life.

Regardless of our choice of door or our WHY, we have free will to choose. Nevertheless, Psalm 40:8 shares the right choice: "*I delight to do Your will, O my God, And Your law is within my heart.*" What makes this such a great choice? It regulates the level of disbursement of our Spiritual Gifts, Creativity, and Blueprint. Is this fair? Absolutely. If we are choosing the wrong doors and are clueless about our WHY, we will mismanage Divine Information, Instructions, and Secrets.

What if we have it going on before men and create a path that suits our wants, needs, and desires? Still, the daunting question is, 'Do we have it going on in the Eye of God?' There is no need for debate here: It is a 'yes' or 'no' question!

Amid trials and tribulations, it can become so easy to lose sight of the hidden potential we possess while feeling lost and uncertain about our next step. Yet, God has always provided a Divine Paper Trail of Provisional Wisdom and Supernatural Intervention if we only establish a *Spirit to Spirit* Relationship, *As It Pleases Him.* Is this the only way? No, it is not! From all walks of life, we will always have the option of going the right way or the wrong way! Plus, the enemy is always ready for our moments of weakness to capitalize on where we have fallen short, become traumatized, lost trust, or lacked faith.

Then again, they are waiting to set us up or ambush us the moment we lack Spiritual Discernment or overlook the wolves in sheep's clothing. How do we know the difference between a wolf and the real deal? *"By their fruits you will know them."* Matthew 7:20.

Now, if one does not know what the Fruits of the Spirit are...then it is time to get in the know! More importantly, if we are operating with rotten or mangled fruits, we will miss the enemy, wolf, or Diamond in the Rough with a Spiritual Woe attached, especially when our loose lips are sinking ships. Is this Biblical? I would have it no other way. *"Woe to those who call evil good, and good evil; Who put darkness for light, and light for darkness; Who put bitter for sweet, and sweet for bitter!"* Isaiah 5:20.

With the Divine Paper Trail, abundance, provision, or liveliness can emerge from even the most inhospitable places, causing the looks of something or someone to become deceiving. Therefore, we must exercise our faith, hope, and love toward the enduring PROMISE written on the Tablet of the Heart, connecting the dots accordingly.

Why must we connect the dots with the Divine Paper Trail? Obedience is one of the determining factors that opens our Creative Mindset. For example, if we do not listen, how can we obey? We cannot! Rebelling inwardly is the same as outward rebellion in the Eye of God.

How does rebellion occur, especially if we do not take action? This concept of non-action works for us in practical everyday living when developing self-control, self-analysis, self-mirroring, and self-correction. But with God, He takes note of our heart postures, leaving room for the chastening of the conceptual factor of rebellion. What does this mean? If rebellion is conceived in the mind, there is a seed relating to something or someone, possibly relating to some form of trauma, conditioning, unforgiveness, or bias. For this reason,

Proverbs 4:23 says, *"Keep your heart with all diligence, for out of it spring the issues of life."*

Why is chastening necessary when dealing with the Divine Paper Trail? Rebellion, deflecting, and disobedience are His soft spots stemming from the Garden of Eden. Does God really have a soft spot? Absolutely! For us, it is called MERCY because if He gave us what we deserved, we would hang our heads down in shame! Therefore, He allows the Vicissitudes and Cycles of Life to make their best attempt to invoke corrective measures without violating anyone's free will. Hebrews 12:6 says, *"For whom the Lord loves He chastens, And scourges every son whom He receives."*

What is the big deal about rebellion, deflecting, and disobedience? They become the fertilizer for all the other negative characteristics, regardless of whether we are sold out to the Kingdom of God, sold out to ourselves, or sold out to another. The bottom line is that rebellion, deflecting, and disobedience pump the brakes on our Creative Mindsets. Why? The mindful gauge is set on debauchery, idolatry, or selfishness.

What if the mindful gauge is NOT set on debauchery, idolatry, or selfishness, but we struggle with rebellion, deflecting, and disobedience? With all due respect, it is fair to say that we would have a problem with lying to ourselves as well.

Why would one have a lying problem? We all have our moments of falling short in this area. By the Grace of God, this is why we need the Holy Spirit to guide us, the Blood of Jesus to cover us, the Fruits of the Spirit to help us, and the Word of God to align us. All of these BREAK the chokehold of jealousy, envy, pride, greed, coveting, and competitiveness that link us to the lust of the eyes, the lust of the flesh, and the pride of life.

What is the benefit of resetting our mind gauges as such? We become trained, *As It Pleases God*, breaking us out of pleasing ourselves and putting a halt to fleshly desires. Hebrews 12:11 says, *"Now no chastening seems to be joyful for the present, but painful; nevertheless, afterward it yields the peaceable fruit of righteousness to those who have been trained by it."*

Nonetheless, when we humbly listen and obey, *As It Pleases God*, here is the Spiritual Seal: *"No temptation has overtaken you except such as is common to man; but God is faithful, who will not allow you to be tempted beyond what you are able, but with the temptation will also make the way of escape, that you may be able to bear it."* 1 Corinthians 10:13.

CHAPTER 7

Creative Mindset

Are you creative? Do you know what creativity does for you? Are you dealing with creative blocks? Then again, do you feel worthy of being creative?

The Power of Creativity is a phenomenal force that resides within each of us, waiting to be heard, unleashed, and used. However, there is a distinction between regular creativity and what we can refer to as Divine Creativity. A Creative Mindset that is rooted in respect and gratitude not only sets us apart from the ordinary. But it also aligns us with the Heavenly of Heavens, allowing us to tap into a Fountain of Inspirational Wisdom that transcends the limitations of conventional thinking, believing, and rationalizing, *As It Pleases God.*

When putting forth the effort to approach creativity with reverence and appreciation, we open the Floodgates of Heaven, allowing the Creative Mindset to bring forth according to our Predestined Blueprint. By positively using this GIFT, we can uplift, inspire, and connect to God, ourselves, and others on a profound level. In addition, we can also cultivate an environment that encourages and supports the free flow of ideas, thoughts, concepts, and artistic endeavors with a diversity of creative and picturesque expressions.

How do we make the difference between DIVINE and normal creativity make sense? Divine Creativity is from God, our Heavenly Father, for our Blueprinted Purpose. When engaging in *Spirit to Spirit* Relations with our Divinely Created Receptors, *As It Pleases Him*, it often removes us from a cycle of déjà vu. In addition, it also places us in a Spiritual Classroom for Spiritual Development and Harmonization.

Meanwhile, fundamental creativity is already prewired within us to survive our Heaven on Earth Experiences along with the Vicissitudes and Cycles of Life. However, it often thrusts us into cycles of déjà vu due to some form of selfishness, disobedience, pompousness, misuse, abuse, or rebellion.

In all simplicity, by respecting the Creator, *As It Pleases Him*, we can glean from His Divine Reservoir, similar to the Woman at the Well, also known as the Samaritan Woman in John 4. What does the Woman at the Well have to do with our Creative Mindset? From my perspective, she had enough creativity to be WILLING to give Jesus a drink of water when He placed a demand on her gift to quench His thirst.

Now, the question is, 'Did Jesus ever take that drink of water from her?' Who knows, right? What we do know is that the desire for Living Water was evident because "*The woman then left her waterpot, went her way into the city, and said to the men, 'Come, see a Man who told me all things that I ever did. Could this be the Christ?' Then they went out of the city and came to Him.*" John 4:28-30.

By developing the WILLINGNESS to override her secret thirsts, needs, or desires to satiate His, it unveiled her HEART POSTURE. As a result, she tapped into a limitless well of ideas, thoughts, and possibilities she would not have had otherwise. Simply put, by unfolding her hand to give, the Spirit of the Lord opened His Divine Hands to bring her in Purpose on purpose.

How did the Samaritan Woman become purposeful after the encounter with Jesus? She became an evangelist to her community. Yes, the same woman and community that were judged, marginalized, or considered outsiders. Her self-expression and encounter were the bridge that God used to connect her with others dealing with the same issues of being an outcast. From that day on, it gave her recognition, respect, and a sense of belonging in the community, allowing her creativity to flourish, bringing people together, and inspiring them to embrace their own unique gifts and respect themselves for who they are. Here are a few things we can glean from the Samaritan Woman, but not limited to such:

- ☐ The woman at the well teaches us about the transformative power of encountering Jesus to experience the overflow of Living Water from the inside out.

- ☐ Her story illustrates the importance of being open to receiving the Spiritual Advice and Nourishment needed to self-correct.

- ☐ The encounter with Jesus shows the value of honest and open communication in our *Spirit to Spirit* Relationship with God.

- ☐ The woman's willingness to faithfully engage in dialogue with Jesus demonstrates the importance of seeking understanding when on our Spiritual Journey.

- ☐ Her story reminds us that Jesus offers Living Water to quench our Spiritual Thirsts hidden under people, places, and things, clouding our sense of sound judgment.

- ☐ The woman's experience highlights the significance of putting aside societal biases or barriers to connect with others using our people skills and not judgmental ones.

- ☐ Her response to Jesus' Divine Revelations emphasizes being open and honest about where we are in our Spiritual Walk.

- ☐ The woman's TESTIMONY serves as a powerful example of how our GIFTS will make room for us.

- ☐ Her encounter with Jesus challenges us to examine our own preconceptions and prejudices in our interactions with others.

- ☐ The woman at the well inspires us to share our faith experiences boldly and respect the testimony of others while doing so.

What does respect have to do with Believers or their mindsets? Before any action is taken, God intricately shapes the creativity of the mind, ensuring that it is in perfect alignment with the heart and hands.

The intricate Spiritual Interplay between the mind, heart, and hands in our actions is a reflection of how God shapes the flow of our creativity. Here is the deal: Before any action takes place, God intricately works within our minds, ensuring that our creativity is in perfect alignment with our hearts and hands. This Divine Orchestration guides us to act in ways that are in harmony with our most authentic selves, Predestined Blueprint, and Divine Expectations set forth by the Heavenly of Heavens.

If our hearts are resistant to the Leading of the Lord, our creativity will become stifled, getting a little bit here and there, similar to having a leaking faucet. Unfortunately, the creativity of the leaky faucet is not what God has in mind for us. Why? It creates an environment where we become creativity bandits or critics.

For example, we have a person who is clueless about what to do. So, they go to a friend for professional guidance, and out of the kindness of this person's heart, they share a roadmap of what needs to occur. Then, this person takes their friend's idea and presents it to those who were equally clueless about what to do prior to. All of a sudden, they take the idea and pick it apart as if they knew what to do in the first place, becoming creativity bandits or critics and making a professional plan a run-of-the-mill one.

As a result, the professional friend refused to sign off, endorse, or engage in the shambles they created. Why would someone help and then turn around to refuse to assist? Their mindsets were different. One was a professional operating with Divine Creativity, priding themselves on Proverbs 22:1. *"A good name is to be chosen rather than great riches, Loving favor rather than silver and gold."* The others were unprofessional and lacked quality and creativity, operating with zero integrity like a putrified ointment in Ecclesiastes 10:1. *"Dead flies putrefy the perfumer's ointment, And cause it to give off a foul odor; So does a little folly to one respected for wisdom and honor."*

The moral of the story is: Before seeking creativity from another, we should force the mind to work for itself, presenting a mindmap or roadmap of what we see in our mind's eye FIRST, building from the ground up. Then, we need to get a second set of eyes to help us perfect what is already there while operating with outright integrity, especially when dealing with a Creative Mindset.

Building Upward

What is the big deal about building from the ground up when we are dealing with creativity? It is not wise to build from the highest common denominator; we must build from the lowest to the highest, creating a stable foundation for our creative efforts. If not, ungratefulness, imbalance, disorder, frailty, and disrespect are added to our equational efforts. How so? When looking from the top down, there will always be a different perspective or view involved than there would be from the ground up. Plus, if we start building a building from the top down, we are in big trouble. Thus, when Building Upward with what we have in our hands with Divine Creativity, we must begin with a solid foundation, focusing on BALANCE and STABILITY.

With a Creative Mindset, the lowest common denominator represents the most basic, universally accessible level of understanding, training, authentication, or appreciation for creative work. On the other hand, striving for the highest common denominator will challenge creators to aim for the most elevated, multifaceted, professional, and sophisticated expressions of doing what they do best. As a result, it brings about perfectionists, idealists, and realists who may crumble under pressure.

Why would some crumble over creativity? It happens all too often; it is just that most do not discuss it openly. Unfortunately, when we have little or no experience in getting our hands dirty (putting in the real work that no one wants to do), we tend to turn up our noses at those appearing beneath us or having less than us. But most often, the hidden creativity will lie within those who are considered to be the lowest common denominator.

For example, I ran into someone who made a statement: 'No one making less than them or having less than them could not tell them anything.' I shook my head in dismay while holding my tongue because he was a pastor. I asked myself, 'How did we get to this point of being deceived beyond measure by human standards and reasonings, especially when God is Spirit?'

This man was preaching from the Holy Bible. He had the nerve to make a statement as such, especially when God's Divine Call is open to all, regardless of our social status, financial status, articulation, degrees, job, or human knowledgeable wisdom. Let me repeat: NO ONE is exempt from becoming usable, according to their Predestined Blueprinted Mission! God will use anything or anyone to accomplish His Divine Purpose.

Here is the deal: The Bible this man uses, better yet, the one we all use, is written by our Forefathers, who had less than us, who still did more, and were used more for the Kingdom of God. Yet, this man was secretly gleaning information from those appearing as the lowest common denominator, deceiving people left and right. Yet he did not realize he was dealing with one of the highest common denominators, built from the ground up with zero fluff.

Unfortunately, he did not realize to whom he was speaking. How can he not know as a Believer? He lacked Spiritual Discernment, allowing his tongue to write checks that his soul could not cash. With outright humility, I did not utter a mumbling word, attempt to defend myself, or debate the Word of God. Why? I had to get this story. The only way to do so is to zip my lips, allowing my tongue to become the pen of a ready writer, allowing my Creative Mindset to get busy doing what I do best.

For the sake of Kingdom Edification, his words, demeanor, character, and people skills unveiled everything I needed to know. He had rotten fruits all over the place, with zero knowledge of how to apply the Fruits of the Spirit or how to behave Christlike. Meanwhile, pimping God with a shyster (deceptive) mentality. And then, putting on a show pretending to be better than the next person with a flaky foundation while trying to convince others, including myself, that it was solid.

In the Eye of God, if our foundation is flaky, solid, faulty, or whatever, OWN IT, work on it, or do something about it WITHOUT whitewashing it with deceptive measures. It is this type of behavior that will cause the Creative Mindset to shut down completely. Once the creative factory comes to a complete halt, we have to use others to keep up the image. However, it does not prevent the psyche from suffering insecurities, unworthiness, or unusability. Still, we should never allow it to get to this point in or out of the Kingdom of God.

When Building Upward, *As It Pleases God*, here are three things we must know to prevent power, money, sex, status, and power from placing a vice grip on our creativity:

- ☐ *"The foolishness of God is wiser than men, and the weakness of God is stronger than men."* 1 Corinthians 1:25. God's all-inclusive and all-encompassing Divine Measures do not lie. He knows more than we do! So, it behooves us to place the Holy Trinity at the forefront of all things.

- ☐ *"For you see your calling, brethren, that not many wise according to the flesh, not many mighty, not many noble, are called."* 1 Corinthians 1:26. God's call is not limited to those who are considered wise, powerful, or noble by worldly standards. He uses Spiritual Standards for those who are WILLING and OBEDIENT. According to the Heavenly of Heavens, the goal is to be used CONTINUALLY. When trusted in this manner, it comes with powerful Spiritual Reinforcement, guaranteed!

- ☐ *"But God has chosen the foolish things of the world to put to shame the wise, and God has chosen the weak things of the world to put to shame the things which are mighty."* 1 Corinthians 1:27. According to the Ancient of Days, Divine Wisdom, Creativity, and Strength transcend human understanding. Always remember God's Divine Ways are not bound by human logic or reasoning; therefore, we must develop a *Spirit to Spirit* Relationship to understand Spiritual Logic and Reasoning *As It Pleases Him*. If not, we are bound to get it or Him all wrong.

Building Upward, *As It Pleases God*, governs whether we will follow instructions or not, which determines or hinders the flow of Divine Information, Strategies, Concepts, and Precepts.

What if we choose not to Build Upward? We have free will to build downward if we like. God does not force us to build anything; we must want it for ourselves. Nevertheless, if we become resistant to following instructions, we become subject to gleaning from another man's reservoir.

Why will we have to glean from others, especially as Believers? Disobedience, rebellion, and arrogance block our authentic Creative Juices or Flow from the Heavenly of Heavens that sometimes make us feel or appear like boo boo the fool. Consequently, this keeps us in the milking stages of Spirituality instead of enjoying Spiritual Meat. Who knows, right? Here is what Hebrews 5:12 says about this matter: *"For though by this time you ought to be teachers, you need someone to teach you again the first principles of the oracles of God; and you have come to need milk and not solid food." "I fed you with milk and not with solid food; for until now you were not able to receive it, and even now you are still not able."* 1 Corinthians 3:2.

What is the big deal about needing Spiritual Milk? There is no big deal; it merely determines our Spiritual Status in the Kingdom of God. Who am I to judge, right? No judgment is intended; we all will pass through this phase. The goal is not to remain there! Here is what Hebrews 5:13 says, *"For everyone who partakes only of milk is unskilled in the word of righteousness, for he is a babe."* Now, if we are unskilled in righteousness, we will lack Spiritual Respect in areas where we should extend it. What does this mean? *Spirit knows Spirit. Spirit respects Spirit.*

Spiritual Respect

Where there is a lack of respect, there is immaturity residing from within. If we are not trained in Spiritual Etiquette from the Heavenly of Heavens, it is an indication that our Spiritual Ranking is lower in the Realm of the Spirit.

What makes someone better than the next person in the Realm of the Spirit? No one is better than anyone because we are ONE in Christ Jesus. However, for those who are Highly Ranked in the Spirit according to the Heavenly of Heavens, we will not know who they are unless the Holy Spirit reveals them to us.

Why would the average person not recognize them? They are humble, selfless, respectful, and kind, needing no accolades and not appearing as what they are. If arrogance, disobedience, debauchery, or unkindness reside, those are a few Spiritual Red Flags that drop our Spiritual Ranking, even if we think we have it going on or we are the best thing since sliced bread.

In all things Spiritual, most often, we pride ourselves on execution or putting the cart before the horse. Unfortunately, this is where we fall short in the Eye of God. In addition, we will also find ourselves misapplying the Blood of Jesus and attempting to misuse the Holy Spirit based on our personal conditioning, perceptions, biases, and judgments. All of this is done without Spiritual Authority or Facts from the Heavenly of Heavens.

For example, we are all known by our fruits, and we have someone appearing Holy-Ghost-Filled and Fire-Baptized sitting next to someone who is also Divinely Anointed. The one proclaiming to be touched by the Holy Spirit is right next to someone who has an extreme sensitivity to someone screaming in their ear, causing them to get a headache instantly. Yet, this person continued to scream at the top of their lungs, disrespecting the person next to them while attempting to convince others that God had touched them.

Some would say the person is right, and some would say they are wrong; however, the Holy Spirit operates decent and in order.

If the Holy Spirit were in full effect, do you think He would not know that this sound would affect or debilitate the person next to them? He knows, and His method of operation would RESPECT the condition of the next man. He provides an environment for everyone to receive, and not just one person who is disrupting the Spiritual Flow with their bodacious conduct, overriding or distracting the frequency of another. Culture, Religion, and Tradition have closed our eyes to the way in which the Holy Spirit operates and disrespects others who bring about order.

Listen, if the Holy Spirit is truly speaking, He will NOT violate the time, place, or others just to be heard, seen, or put on a show. Nor does LOUDNESS move Him. Really? Yes, really. Sound is a frequency sent forth from the Heavenly of Heavens regardless of the volume. Blasphemy, right? Wrong! Connecting to the Holy Spirit is not about volume or loudness, as most would think. It is about vibration...A Spiritual Vibration, to be exact. Psalm 19:3 says, *"There is no speech nor language where their voice is not heard."* *"The voice of the Lord is over the waters; the God of glory thunders; the Lord is over many waters."* Psalm 29:3.

Here is where we veer into Spiritual Error: Revelation 1:10 says, *"I was in the Spirit on the Lord's Day, and I heard behind me a loud voice, as of a trumpet."* From our perspective, we associate this loud voice with our external ears, but it is heard through our Spiritual Ears. In my opinion, this is similar to how animals communicate, plan, and maneuver without saying one audible word that we can hear, understand, articulate, or reproduce, while having us pegged. To say the least, if our Spiritual Ears are NOT developed, *As It Pleases God*, we will NOT hear the Voice, Trumpet, or Instructions, regardless of the racket we are making in Earthen Vessels.

Is our prayer considered racket? Is this not disrespectful? Perhaps, but it depends on who is offended because *"Dishonest scales are an abomination to the Lord, but a just weight is His delight."* Proverbs 11:1. In all simplicity, the only ones who may become offended by the word racket are those who are making it. Why is this the case in the Eye of God? Those who can call forth a Legion of Angels at the drop of a dime are not worried about making a racket. They are more concerned about adequately governing their Spiritual Anointing and Power, *As It Pleases God*, to avoid its misuse, abuse, or backfire. Is this Biblical? Of course. I would have it no other way. Proverbs 16:11 says, *"Honest weights and scales are the Lord's; all the weights in the bag are His work."* And, *"Diverse weights and diverse measures, they are both alike, an abomination to the Lord."* Proverbs 20:10.

Amid developing a Respectful Mindset, *As It Pleases God*, we must understand what He considers diverse weights, measures, and scales because they may vary from person to person, situation to situation, trauma to trauma, bias to bias, culture to culture, and so on. Why must we go to Him on this matter? He knows us better than we know ourselves. Plus, no one knows Him better than Him, nor do they know our Predestined Blueprint better than Him; thus, it behooves us to go to the Source, *Spirit to Spirit*.

For the record, no one, and I mean no one, has God fully pegged. He will change the Spiritual Language at a moment's notice, giving us a Tower of Babel Experience to the point where we do not know if we are coming or going. For this reason, it is time out for the lies about man doing what only God can do through the use of the Holy Spirit and the covering of the Blood of Jesus as Spiritual Atonement for us. Then again, we can walk around playing God, hooping and hollering because we like to be seen by men, but rest assured, a rude awakening is on the horizon that will begin within the human psyche.

What is the big deal about hooping and hollering for the Lord? We have free will to do whatever, whenever, and however when worshipping the Lord. Nevertheless, "*Let nothing be done through selfish ambition or conceit, but in lowliness of mind let each esteem others better than himself.*" Philippians 2:3. But we must never forget, "*Death and life are in the power of the tongue, and those who love it will eat its fruit.*" Proverbs 18:21.

To add insult to injury, those who engage in negative behaviors to be seen or who seek attention are categorized as those who are easily offended, lack creativity, avoid humility, and fall short in the execution process. So, they find people to use or do their bidding for them, and they are known to consume their own fruits without sharing them, *As It Pleases God*.

Why is this such a big deal in the Eye of God? Is this not judging? Maybe or maybe not, but to get to the root of an issue, it must be exposed for what it is. Nor will I sit back and sugarcoat a matter that has placed us in the predicament we are in today, and what needs our attention. Here are a few items to look for when pinpointing the root, but not limited to such:

- ☐ Pay attention to recurring patterns of behavior.
- ☐ Take note of negative thoughts or inner chatter.
- ☐ Look for signs of defensiveness.
- ☐ Look at the reluctance to accept responsibility.
- ☐ Notice consistent negative attitudes or pessimism.
- ☐ Identify excessive criticism.
- ☐ Pay attention to judgmental words or behaviors.
- ☐ Monitor reactions to stress or frustration.
- ☐ Observe communication styles and languages.
- ☐ Take note of sarcasm or passive-aggressive remarks.
- ☐ Watch for signs of manipulation.
- ☐ Pay attention to the area of dishonesty.
- ☐ Take note of where the lack of humility exists.

- ☐ Consider the impact of negative behaviors on others.
- ☐ Look for patterns of blame-shifting.
- ☐ Notice excessive self-criticism.
- ☐ Pay close attention to areas of low self-esteem.
- ☐ Identify consistent patterns of procrastination.
- ☐ Pay attention to avoidances.
- ☐ Watch for signs of aggression or hostility.
- ☐ Notice patterns of disrespect towards others.
- ☐ Observe habits of complaining.
- ☐ Identify self-sabotage or undermining behaviors.
- ☐ Monitor reactions to change or new challenges.
- ☐ Look for signs of entitlement or selfish behaviors.

With this checklist, we can proactively prepare ourselves with the Fruit Inspection needed to get off Spiritual Milk to enjoy the Spiritual Meat from the Heavenly of Heavens we are entitled to.

Chapter 8

Fruit Inspection

The Spiritual Inspections from the Heavenly of Heavens have been avoided from the onset of our existence, bringing us to where we are today. Although our Forefathers prepared the way for us, we often miss out on the Fruit Inspections required for the prepackaging of our NEWNESS in Christ Jesus. Of course, we all have our Predestined Blueprint hidden within us; however, the prepackaging of the Blood of Jesus is needed for our Spiritual Atonement to cover us in the pre-inspection (prior to being saved) and post-inspection (recovering from backsliding) phases.

What about the current Fruit Inspection phase? There is no current phase without proper USE. And if we are currently using them, *As It Pleases God*, it means that the HOLY SPIRIT must provide REAL-TIME corrective measures. So, what are we doing now? I am preparing you to use the Fruits of the Spirit, *As It Pleases God*.

Why is preparation necessary? If we were using them properly, *As It Pleases Him*, I would not be here! Is this not a little arrogant? No, it is Time-Appointed and Time-Appropriated from the Ancient of Days.

When we consume our own fruits out of selfishness, the Cycles and Vicissitudes of Life begin to see us as a canker sore, thrusting us into a cycle of déjà vu. How can we make this make sense in layman's terms? Proverbs 18:20 says,

"A man's stomach shall be satisfied from the fruit of his mouth; From the produce of his lips he shall be filled." Simply put, what comes out of our mouths is a portion of the fruits we are sharing. Proverbs 12:14 says, "A man will be satisfied with good by the fruit of his mouth, And the recompense of a man's hands will be rendered to him."

Our actions and what we are doing, saying, and becoming are considered a portion of our fruits, contributing to whether we are considered a Tree of Life or a Tree of Death. Then again, it will also determine whether we will build up people, places, and things or whether we will break them down to their lowest common denominator, using them up for our benefit.

What is the big deal about fruits as a Believer? The deal is that: "*A wholesome tongue is a tree of life, But perverseness in it breaks the spirit.*" Proverbs 15:4. If we are broken, we must check our fruits. If we are operating in wholeness, we still must check and monitor our fruits while inspecting those of another to protect our own. Why? One bad fruit can spoil the whole bunch. So, we must know about fruits from a Divine Perspective to know when to hold, fold, or walk away with clean hands and a pure heart.

What are the Fruits of the Spirit? "*But the fruit of the Spirit is love, joy, peace, longsuffering (patience), kindness, goodness, faithfulness, gentleness, self-control. Against such there is no law.*" Galatians 5:22-23. These are powerful virtues representing the PRESENCE of the Holy Spirit in one's life, and they keep Him from lying dormant.

According to the Heavenly of Heavens, the Fruits of the Spirit embody the essence of Kingdom Poshness, the chosen Spiritual Etiquette for our Earthen Vessels. Now, to prepare ourselves for the FILLING or the INDWELLING of the Holy Spirit, we must selflessly engage, *As It Pleases God.*

Can we engage the Holy Spirit without God? No, the Holy Spirit comes as a package deal called the Holy Trinity (The Father, Son, and Holy Spirit). Now, we can engage other Spirits, but there are consequences, repercussions, and other sacrifices required for engaging. Simply put, there is a right and wrong way in all things...but with God Almighty, it is best to choose the right way. Whether we believe in the Holy Trinity or not, it is what it is, and we, as lesser Spiritual Beings, cannot change this Divine Order.

What does the Indwelling of the Holy Spirit mean? *"Do you not know that you are the temple of God and that the Spirit of God dwells in you?"* 1 Corinthians 3:16. Why do we need this as Believers? *"But you are not in the flesh but in the Spirit, if indeed the Spirit of God dwells in you. Now if anyone does not have the Spirit of Christ, he is not His."* Romans 8:9. *"Or do you not know that your body is the temple of the Holy Spirit who is in you, whom you have from God, and you are not your own?"* 1 Corinthians 6:19.

The Fruits of the Spirit, be it personal, private, professional, or communal, are underrated, suppressed, and often ignored by those who do not truly understand them, *As It Pleases God.* For a time such as this, please allow me to break them down with a formal Fruit Inspection. Why must a Fruit Inspection take place, especially when we have all of our ducks in a row? I am not here to count anyone's duckies or flunkies and how they came to be. I am here to ensure the Indwelling of the Holy Spirit can be properly AWAKENED, *As It Pleases God.*

Love Inspection

Love in its purest form is a sweet-smelling aroma in the Heavenly of Heavens, exposing the imitators and player-haters. Why must we exhibit love? We have free will to choose love or hate, and there is no neutral option unless it is neutral love or neutral hate. Proverbs 10:12 says, *"Hatred stirs up strife, but love covers all sins."*

Love encompasses compassion, empathy, and selflessness. The option should always be: *"Walk in love, as Christ also has* loved us and given Himself for us, an offering and a sacrifice to God for a sweet-smelling aroma." Ephesians 5:2.

Love is the common ingredient in all of the Fruits of the Spirit. Unfortunately, it is also the ingredient often left out of the mix of our personal lives, professional tidings, social camaraderies, and Spiritual Well-Being.

Why is love left out when we are indeed loving people, and we have people who absolutely love and adore us? Being a loving or adored person has little to do with love, *As It Pleases God*.

The truth of the matter is that we love to please ourselves and those around us with conditions attached, called conditional love. When the conditions are right, we love. On the other hand, if the conditions are unpleasant or unpleasing, we turn our love off, like flipping a light switch. Blasphemy, right? Wrong! Look at the divorce rate! It is at an 80% failure rate; therefore, something in the love mix is not right, especially in the Eye of God. But the question remains, 'Why is love making a fool out of us?'

To be clear, no one is exempt from the factors of conditional love and how it affects, infects, traumatizes, or trains us. However, with the Fruit Inspection, we must put it into its proper perspective, *As It Pleases God*, and not to please ourselves with little or no understanding. Here is what Hosea 4:6 has to say about this matter: *"My people are destroyed for lack of knowledge. Because you have rejected knowledge, I also will reject you from being priest for Me; because you have forgotten the law of your God, I also will forget your children."*

What do we need to understand as Believers, and what do our children have to do with our misunderstandings? We need to understand the Fruits of the Spirit and how they are needed to make love work. If we do not learn, we prevent our children, whom we claim to love, from getting a head start on learning what we should have.

Unawaringly, we make our children suffer, work harder, or pull double duty to understand, unravel, or continue the cycle of what we NEGLECTED to do, learn, understand, and share. For this reason, and the love I have for all mankind, the buck stops here on the neglect and misunderstandings of the Fruits of the Spirit!

Love is one of the most misunderstood emotional commodities known to mankind because we often associate love with power, money, sex, status, and fame. All of which thrust us into a state of idolatry in the Eye of God without realizing we are there. Then again, it may keep us looking for love in all the wrong places to fill a void or hole that only the Holiness of God can fill.

If we do a conditional Love Inspection on ourselves, we will find that conditions are leading us based on our wants, needs, and desires that may or may not be a part of the Divine Plan. Still, it is our responsibility to determine whether they are or are not a part of it. Therefore, we must add God into our equations, *Spirit to Spirit*, to understand the difference between conditional love, safe love, unsafe love, tough love, and love at a distance. All of these may mean something different to all of us depending on our mindsets, thoughts, traumas, biases, conditioning, and the training needed.

Why would we need training on love differences as Believers? It is not man's way of training, as most would think. It is Spiritual Training, to be exact.

The Spiritual Classroom is used in many instances to get our emotions, mindsets, and psyche in check; however, listed below are a few Spiritual Training Sessions that will take place under the Love Inspection Forum, but not limited to such:

- ☐ Training for our Predestined Blueprint, *As It Pleases God*.
- ☐ Spiritually Tilling our own grounds, *As It Pleases God*.
- ☐ Polishing our Spiritual Fruits, *As It Pleases God*.

- ☐ Building Christlike Character, *As It Pleases God.*
- ☐ Becoming Spirit-Led, *As It Pleases God.*
- ☐ Building our people skills, *As It Pleases God.*
- ☐ Pruning process, *As It Pleases God.*
- ☐ Transitioning from our old to new, *As It Pleases God.*
- ☐ Transitioning to our NEXT, *As It Pleases God.*
- ☐ Spiritually Purging, *As It Pleases God.*

Why do we need Spiritual Training Sessions in the Love Inspection Forum? It divides our selfless love from our selfish love. What does this mean? There is no training needed to please ourselves or do our own thing.

Why is no training needed to please ourselves? Because when our feelings lead us, we tend to go with the flow, making up our own rules as we go, with little or no self-control due to the perceived benefits associated. Often, the self-led, ungoverned flow of love leads us straight into the PIT with a one-way ticket due to becoming unwise, soul-tied, traumatized, abused, or unequally yoked due to power, money, sex, status, and fame.

Why would we have a one-way ticket into the PIT? We often do not know that we have the AUTHORITY to cancel the ticket, nor do we know WHAT TO DO to reverse it. As a result, we opt to handle things on our own without adding the Holy Trinity into our equational efforts.

But all hope is not lost in the Love Inspection. Regardless of where we are or where our tickets have us headed, repeat Psalm 40:2 over and over to get our conscience or Spiritual Compass back on track, *As It Pleases God.* It says, *"He also brought me up out of a horrible pit, out of the miry clay, and set my feet upon a rock, and established my steps."* And then claim this scripture: *"O Lord, You brought my soul up from the grave; You have kept me alive, that I should not go down to the pit."* Psalm 30:3.

Will Psalm 40:2 and Psalm 30:3 help us? They will do more for you than the PIT will ever do. So, use it before you lose it! We will discuss the positive and negative hormonal impacts later in this chapter.

Amid all, before we move to the Joy Inspection, know this: *"And now abide faith, hope, love, these three; but the greatest of these is love."* 1 Corinthians 13:13.

Joy Inspection

Joy emanates from within with an internal anchor, bringing a sense of inner contentment with the uncertainties we face daily. With the ever-changing situations and long list of adversities, we must regain our solitude to avoid losing our marbles due to the issues of life.

Unbeknown to most, joy can coexist with other emotions, including sadness, anger, anxiety, and fear. How can they coexist? Joy does not stop us from feeling how we feel; it is designed to nurse us through our thoughts, emotions, or contemplations. Then again, it may lessen the time spent dealing with them. Regardless of our outward circumstances or the ups and downs of life, we all have access to and equal rights to joy. No one is exempt from its use, nor should we deprive anyone of it.

How can we deprive anyone of joy when it comes from within? When we deprive someone of their peace, whitewash their perspectives, bully them, violate their free will, or intentionally make their lives difficult, we can contribute to the deprivation of joy. How do we make this make sense? The deprivation is accomplished through what is called invokable discontentment or invoking hardship and pain upon someone, making them a victim. In all simplicity, it is intentional victimization or hardship.

Still, no one can take the gift of joy unless we willfully surrender it from within to the woe-unto-me victim mentality. However, we do not want to contribute to someone willfully surrendering because of our negative behaviors, words, or whatever.

Why should we exercise caution? It can cause us to forfeit our joy, similar to how King Saul lost his joy in 1 Samuel. The loss of it may remain until repentance, apology, or forgiveness occurs on our behalf or another. If we avoid doing so, disobedience can lead to us becoming increasingly paranoid, jealous, envious, prideful, covetous, and competitive. Can this really happen due to the lack of joy? It is happening right before our very eyes, in plain sight. For this reason, we must exercise extreme caution when engaging in such a manner.

The goal of the Joy Inspection is to make people victorious by spreading peace, love, understanding, and contentment. According to the Heavenly of Heavens, most of us do not know what joy is and what it is not. We often confuse joy and happiness to be one and the same, but they are not. Joy is experienced from within (intangibly) and is not contingent upon external factors such as success, wealth, status, or relationships.

Meanwhile, happiness, on the other hand, is experienced externally or tangibly from people, places, and things. Happiness is linked to our Earthen Vessels for our Heaven on Earth Experiences. Simply put, it is action form or performance-driven, connecting to our senses or the things we can see, feel, touch, hear, and taste, catering to the Mind, Body, Soul, and Spirit. *"Happy is the man who finds wisdom, and the man who gains understanding."* Proverbs 3:13.

Joy is linked to our Spiritual Being of faith, belief, and hope of things we cannot see: *"Therefore with joy you will draw water from the wells of salvation."* Isaiah 12:3. All of these are also associated with the CONDITION of the mindset, thoughts, and heart posture of an individual. For this reason, it behooves us to keep them set on positive.

Why must we remain positive to keep our joy joyous? Negativity drains us. "*A merry heart does good, like medicine, but a broken spirit dries the bones.*" Proverbs 17:22. Does this mean that being joyful can help us heal, Mentally, Physically, Emotionally, and Spiritually? Absolutely! Whereas the lack of it can make us sick, Mentally, Physically, Emotionally, and Spiritually.

How do we know if we are joyful? It will vary from person to person, situation to situation, trauma to trauma, conditioning to conditioning, and so on. Nevertheless, the psyche will always know the truth about our joyfulness and the lack thereof. Here are a few indications, but not limited to such:

- ☐ Smiling for no reason.
- ☐ Not easily provoked.
- ☐ Allow people to be who they are.
- ☐ Feeling grateful for the little things.
- ☐ Having a positive outlook on life.
- ☐ Enjoying the present moment.
- ☐ Being kind and compassionate towards others.
- ☐ Finding pleasure in simple activities.
- ☐ Feeling energized and enthusiastic.
- ☐ Being open to new experiences.
- ☐ Laughing easily.
- ☐ Having a sense of inner peace.
- ☐ Being resilient in the face of challenges.
- ☐ Feeling connected to others.
- ☐ Experiencing a sense of purpose.
- ☐ Being generous and giving.
- ☐ Feeling content with what you have.
- ☐ Being optimistic about the future.
- ☐ Having a sense of fulfillment.
- ☐ Being playful and lighthearted.
- ☐ Embracing your true self.

☐ Spreading joy to others.

How do we make joy make sense? Making joy 'make sense' involves understanding and appreciating its dynamics. It also revolves around finding ways to cultivate and appreciate it through natural resources, such as connecting to nature, spending time with loved ones, enjoying a beautiful sunset, or achieving a personal goal.

Here is the deal: For the restoration or the flourishing of joy, repeat Psalm 51:12 over and over: *"Restore to me the joy of Your salvation, And uphold me by Your generous Spirit."*

Peace Inspection

Peace refers to a state of tranquility and harmony, both within oneself and with others. In addition, it also links our joy with it, like an ironclad combination, giving us hope amid whatever with whomever. Here is the ironclad Spiritual Seal: *"Now may the God of hope fill you with all joy and peace in believing, that you may abound in hope by the power of the Holy Spirit."* Romans 15:13.

Even when chaos and confusion are all around us, we do not have to give in to it or come into an agreement with it, them, or that. *"Depart from evil and do good; seek peace and pursue it."* Psalm 34:14.

How do we depart from evil when it stares us right in the face? Here is the deal: If we reject negativity, reverse it to something positive, pinpoint the win-win or lesson, document it, and give thanks for the experience, we can regain our peace and ONENESS. Here is what Colossians 3:15 tells us: *"Let the peace of God rule in your hearts, to which also you were called in one body; and be thankful."*

What if someone disrupts our peace? No one can disrupt our peace unless we permit them to do so, or we do not know how to regain it once disrupted. In addition, if we lose our peace easily, we can easily lose our joy as well. They are connected. Colossians 1:11 says, *"For this reason we also, since the day we heard it, do not cease to pray for you, and to ask that you may be filled with the knowledge of His will in all wisdom and spiritual understanding; that you may walk worthy of the Lord, fully pleasing Him, being fruitful in every good work and increasing in the knowledge of God; strengthened with all might, according to His glorious power, for all patience and longsuffering with joy."* Colossians 1:9-11.

When we usher in joy, we must align the Spirit of Peace to calm the Mind, Body, Soul, and Spirit. If not, the Spirit of Unrest will do what it does best. What is that? Shake us to the core.

Clearly, people will shoot their shots at bringing unrest and contention into our lives, but we have the authority to accept or decline the invitation. Even if our lives are filled with chaos, stress, and uncertainty, it does not exempt us from holding on to peacefulness. Nor does it prevent us from detaching ourselves from the worries that have a bullseye on our sanity.

Can we really hold on to our peace? Absolutely. It is our God-Given right to hold on to it based on this Spiritual Seal: *"Peace I leave with you; my peace I give you. I do not give to you as the world gives. Do not let your hearts be troubled and do not be afraid."* John 14:27. If we lay claim to this, *As It Pleases God*, then the Spirit of Peace must come forth. Really? Yes, really. *"The Lord gives strength to his people; the Lord blesses his people with peace."* Psalm 29:11. All we need to do is come into AGREEMENT with it, *As It Pleases Him.*

The only question we must ask is, 'Are we His People?" If we are, then we are entitled to place a Spiritual Demand on our peace based on this scripture: *"Blessed are the peacemakers, for they will be called children of God."* Matthew 5:9.

What if we are not God's people? Then, we cannot place a Spiritual Demand on peace. Then again, if we do, it may become like heaping coals on our heads unless we *"Turn from evil and do good; seek peace and pursue it."* Psalm 34:14.

What if we do not do good or seek peace? According to Isaiah 24:10, *"The city of confusion is broken down; Every house is shut up, so that none may go in."* Gaining peace from within requires self-reflection and analysis to understand our thoughts, emotions, traumas, reactions, and behaviors to allow personal growth and self-awareness. Why do we need to reflect from the inside out, *As It Pleases God*? *"When a man's ways please the Lord, he makes even his enemies to be at peace with him."* Proverbs 16:7.

At face value, amid the Peace Inspection phase, we must value being peaceful with God, ourselves, and others to prevent disorder or chaos from lingering or setting up shop within the psyche. Why must we adhere to this as Believers? *"Whoever has no rule over his own spirit is like a city broken down, without walls."* Proverbs 25:28. Once we are chaotic from within, our environment will follow suit with some form of desolation that we may cover up with something else.

What is the something else? It may vary from person to person, situation to situation, trauma to trauma, condition to condition, and so on. Still, it will fall into the categories relating to the lust of the eyes, the lust of the flesh, and the pride of life. All of which leads to a hidden sense of brokenness, void, thirst, and alienation with soothing layers of power, money, sex, fame, or status to coax the longing.

Nevertheless, when the mask comes off or when behind closed doors, the hidden beast comes full circle. Simply put, we can run, but we cannot hide from ourselves. According to the Heavenly of Heavens, true and lasting peace requires us to confront the hidden beast from within, making the pursuit of it more crucial than ever.

What if we do not have a beast from within? Unfortunately, the nature of the beast is within us all, called human nature, representing evil, chaos, temptation, and moral challenges. The moment we think this does not exist, we will get got by the enemy's wiles. Here is what James 1:12-15 says about this matter: *"Blessed is the man who endures temptation; for when he has been approved, he will receive the crown of life which the Lord has promised to those who love Him. Let no one say when he is tempted, 'I am tempted by God'; for God cannot be tempted by evil, nor does He Himself tempt anyone. But each one is tempted when he is drawn away by his own desires and enticed. Then, when desire has conceived, it gives birth to sin; and sin, when it is full-grown, brings forth death."*

We must acknowledge our thoughts, biases, weaknesses, idiosyncrasies, traumas, desires, habits, and fears to prevent the enemy from zapping our peace by hitting us below the belt in our sensitive areas. Thus, if we own our truth and become a work-in-progress, *As It Pleases God*, we can begin to dismantle the negative barriers by understanding that *"For each one shall bear his own load."* Galatians 6:5.

For sure, everyone is in need of work, and if we are working on ourselves, *As It Pleases God*, using the Fruits of the Spirit and behaving Christlike, then He will do what He said that He would do based on our Predestined Blueprinted Mission. How do we make this make sense? Everyone has specific instructions for their Heaven on Earth Experience, which is between the Holy of Holies and the carrier (which is us). We must do our part, and God will do His.

If we do not know what the Divine Instructions are, then it is time to seek a *Spirit to Spirit* Connection with our Heavenly Father to gain Spiritual Access to what is already. Unfortunately, I cannot give instructions, but I can Divinely Illuminate the way. In the meantime, here are a few ways to establish peace from the inside out, but not limited to such:

- ☐ Develop a *Spirit to Spirit* Relationship.
- ☐ Become ONE with the Holy Spirit.
- ☐ Cover yourself with the Blood of Jesus.
- ☐ You must pray for peace.

- ☐ Practice self-reflection and self-awareness.
- ☐ Understand your real thoughts, desires, and emotions.
- ☐ Cultivate empathy and compassion.
- ☐ Engage in open and honest communication.
- ☐ Seek understanding of yourself and others.
- ☐ Create common ground in conflicts.
- ☐ Respect the differences between yourself and others.
- ☐ Foster a sense of connection with others.
- ☐ Embrace diversity.
- ☐ Celebrate the uniqueness of others.
- ☐ Practice mercy and forgiveness.
- ☐ Sincerely REPENT often.
- ☐ Let go of grudges, competitiveness, and resentment.
- ☐ Cultivate a sense of gratitude.
- ☐ Actively listen to others without judgment.
- ☐ Do not interrupt others.
- ☐ Be respectful at all times.
- ☐ Encourage peaceful resolutions.
- ☐ Practice positive negotiation.
- ☐ Promote equality and justice.
- ☐ Engage in acts of kindness.
- ☐ Share to build others positively.
- ☐ Lead by example.
- ☐ Use the Fruits of the Spirit.
- ☐ Spread positivity and love.
- ☐ Reverse negatives into positives.
- ☐ Create a win-win out of everything.
- ☐ Remain on a learning curve to become better.
- ☐ Rejoice in the good, bad, or indifferent.

In peace, here is the Spiritual Decree: *"Aspire to lead a quiet life, to mind your own business, and to work with your own hands, as we commanded you, that you may walk properly toward those who are outside, and that you may lack nothing."* 1 Thessalonians 4:11-12.

Patience Inspection

Patience is a virtue that allows the Spirit of Calmness to permeate our lives amid doing what we do in Earthen Vessels. In dealing with the Vicissitudes and Cycles of Life, we must endure or overcome trials and tribulations with perseverance, tenacity, resilience, and, most of all, patience.

Unbeknown to most, it is patience in the Spiritual Tilling and Pruning process that gets us properly trained and equipped to do what we have been called to do. Plus, it prevents us from being thrown into a cycle of déjà vu with an impatient yoke or oppressive training guide for the areas of impatience, disobedience, lukewarmness, or rebellion.

In the Patience Inspection process, all of our cycles will deal with repentance, forgiveness, mercy, debauchery, hatefulness, pompousness, negativity, unrighteousness, and the lack of understanding. Why must we deal with these things as Believers? They thrust us into the lust of the eyes, the lust of the flesh, the pride of life, and full-blown idolatry without us realizing the underlying strongholds attached.

Whatever we engage in that is not good for us, others, or the Kingdom of God, we should not engage in, especially without adding the Holy Trinity into the equation. Is any of this Biblical? *"And we urge you, brethren, to recognize those who labor among you, and are over you in the Lord and admonish you, and to esteem them very highly in love for their work's sake. Be at peace among yourselves. Now we exhort you, brethren, warn those who are unruly, comfort the fainthearted, uphold the weak, be patient with all. See that no one renders evil for evil to anyone, but always pursue what is good both for yourselves and for all."* 1 Thessalonians 5:12-15.

In the Eye of God, respecting and supporting each other is ideal to maintain harmony, unity, and oneness without throwing each other under the bus. What if we are thrown under the bus by others? We must remain patient and kind amid all with dedication and commitment to feed God's sheep, even if we feel they are not worthy to be fed.

When dealing with the silver lining of patience, we cannot pick and choose who deserves the mercy of God and who does not. In the same way that God was patient with us, we must also be patient with others without showing them a bad face. Clearly, this does not mean getting downright dirty with them or agreeing with them behaving badly. Nonetheless, it does mean that we do not drag them through the mud, especially when we are all made out of it. According to the Heavenly of Heavens, it is God's job to deal with them the way He sees fit; thus, we must stop trying to do His job with the Uzzah mentality.

Who is Uzzah? In the book of 2 Samuel 6:1-7, Uzzah reached out his hand to steady the Ark of the Covenant when the oxen stumbled. As a result, God's anger burned against Uzzah, and he died there beside the ark. Although sad, this story serves as a reminder of the HOLINESS of God, getting out of His way, and the need to approach Him with reverence and obedience when He is working on us, them, or that. All in all, it also illustrates the importance of following God's instructions without hesitation, using Spiritual Discernment, and not taking His presence lightly.

Who, besides God Almighty, knew the thoughts, desires, secrets, underlying mud, or brewing debauchery of Uzzah before touching the Ark of the Covenant? Was all of this negativity, judgment, or condemnatory factors against King David, or was it against God Almighty? The answer to this question will forever remain a mystery. But whatever it was, it was enough to be struck by God and not survive. Yet and still, it serves as a valuable reminder of touching the people, places, and things that truly belong to Him, or when desiring to turn His THEOCRACY (A God-Ruled Nation) into a circus or to make a mockery of Him with a form of godliness.

What does the form of godliness have to do with the Patience Inspection? It is the form used that will cause our patience to come under attack or zap our power, even when pretending to possess this character trait. *"For men will be lovers of themselves, lovers of money, boasters, proud, blasphemers, disobedient to parents, unthankful, unholy, unloving, unforgiving, slanderers, without self-control, brutal, despisers of good, traitors, headstrong, haughty, lovers of pleasure rather than lovers of God, having a form of godliness but denying its power. And from such people turn away!"* 2 Timothy 3:2-5.

Turning away does not mean for us not to use the Fruits of the Spirit or not to behave Christlike. Nor does it mean to turn up our noses and shun people. Why should we not outcast or ostracize others? We do not know what or who God is using or training to fulfill the Spiritual Covenants or bring Divine Alignment, without Spiritual Discernment, *As It Pleases Him*.

Suppose there is any remnant associated with selfishly pleasing ourselves or not doing what we were called to do. In this case, it behooves us to encourage the fainthearted, uphold the weak, offer mercy, and be patient with all. If we are selfish in any way, shape, or form, if we do not know how to use the Fruits of the Spirit, and if we do not know our Divine Blueprint, it means that we HAVE NOT arrived in the Eye of God. Therefore, we should not kick our brothers or sisters when they are down or kick dirt in their faces as if we are squeaky clean. Besides, in the Eye of God, even if we have a little dirt or a lot of it, it is still DIRT.

Why should we not treat people like they treated us? Then my question would be, 'Is it going to make us feel better about ourselves, or will it make us just like them?' Peaceful and respectful interactions are required of us, and if we fail to go after that one sheep that has strayed away, how can we proclaim to be a Shepherd for the Kingdom of God, upholding the weak? For this reason, Galatians 6:9 says, *"And let us not grow weary while doing good, for in due season we shall reap if we do not lose heart."*

Why is patience associated with fruits? Frankly, this is how God deals with us. It is through fruits, seasons, and cycles that life prevails in us and through us. If we do not have them, we do not eat! We, and everything around us, will suffer famine without them.

Remember, it takes crushed and rotten (fermented) grapes to release their juices to make fine wine with time! *"Nor do they put new wine into old wineskins, or else the wineskins break, the wine is spilled, and the wineskins are ruined. But they put new wine into new wineskins, and both are preserved."* Matthew 9:17.

Then again, for those who frown on wine, we can use the olive instead. The powerful lesson of the olive tree is that the olive must be crushed to extract the oil associated with personal growth, social growth, and Spiritual Growth. Refinement of the Olive Tree Anointing takes patience to become something truly extraordinary. Why is refinement necessary? In order to release the most PRECIOUS BLESSINGS of peace, wisdom, and prosperity, one must be willing to endure the crushing and pressing with patience, perseverance, and proactiveness without sitting around twiddling their thumbs.

How do we not twiddle our thumbs when life is lifing? First, we must respect the PLAN of God, *As It Pleases Him*. Secondly, we must learn and understand the lessons associated with the cycle, season, seed, root, or whatever. Thirdly, we must willingly transform or evolve into our next, *As It Pleases Him*, without kicking, screaming, fussing, fighting, or complaining. Fourthly, we must selflessly become prepared to empower another once emerging from adversity, hardship, discomfort, oppression, and struggle.

In the Fruit Inspection process, *As It Pleases God*, we do not prepare to come out of whatever, whenever, however, with whomever empty-handed. When we come out of our Egypt, we must develop the mindset to come out with Divine Provisions for the Divine Promise and Spiritual Journey.

In our resilience and bringing forth qualities such as compassion, empathy, understanding, and wisdom, *As It Pleases God*, we will become a source of empowerment and inspiration to those we encounter along the way. Here is what James 5:7-8 shares: *"Therefore be patient, brethren, until the coming of the Lord. See how the farmer waits for the precious fruit of the earth, waiting patiently for it until it receives the early and latter rain. You also be patient. Establish your hearts, for the coming of the Lord is at hand."*

Kindness Inspection

Kindness in the Eye of God is the critical 'Four For One' Spiritual Gold for our well-being. How is this possible? When you perform acts of kindness, the body has the potential to release four major chemical neurotransmitters that contribute to becoming and remaining a better person, *As It Pleases Him*.

Before we go any deeper, the question is, 'What are chemical neurotransmitters?' In alignment with our DNA, chemical neurotransmitters are essential for communication within the nervous system. They transmit signals between neurons, allowing the brain and body to function properly. These chemical messengers play crucial roles in regulating mood, cognition, movement, and various bodily functions. Imbalances in neurotransmitter levels can contribute to conditions such as depression, anxiety, and other diseases.

How do we make all of this make sense? We must understand that kindness is not a standalone character trait. In the Eye of God, kindness is used in conjunction with love. More importantly, it is also used as a conduit to counteract the lack of love, attention, and affection to preserve the lives of those who are knowingly or unknowingly deprived in some way.

Why is love used as a conjunctioning factor for kindness? Not only is there a physical bonding of love and kindness. It contains a Spiritual and CHEMICAL bonding edifice associated with them. There is a reason why Jeremiah 31:3 says, "*The Lord has appeared of old to me, saying: 'Yes, I have loved you with an everlasting love; Therefore with lovingkindness I have drawn you.'* " In the same way that Jeremiah was drawn with lovingkindness bonded together, we have the same bonding components within us from the Ancient of Days.

According to the Heavenly of Heavens, it is love that can build us, and the lack of it can break us down to the core if we allow it to do so or if we do not apply Spiritual Principles, *As It Pleases God*. What is the purpose of adding God to our love or kindness factors? All of the problems or issues we will face will be centered around the love bonding factors, the lack of it leading to some form of rejection, and the disappointments or failed expectations associated.

More importantly, love is desired by all, even if we pretend we do not need it, do not want it, are embarrassed by it, or refuse to give it. According to the Heavenly of Heavens, it is prewired into our DNA to connect us to the elements of kindness to balance the psyche. How so? It is what is hidden within our psyche that brings out the best and worst in us, or gives way to the mask covering our shamefulness. And it is through our acts of genuine kindness that we can provide a Spiritual Safety Net for ourselves, *As It Pleases God*.

In the Kindness Inspection, we must understand that NO medical intervention can heal a broken heart or broken psyche, even if we seek treatment. However, interjecting willful kindness into our healing regimen can kick-start the healing process when there is a perceived love deficit. No one outside of ourselves can do this for us...We must Spiritually Till our own grounds when it comes down to internal healing.

What about God healing us? If we do not embrace healing, then His Divine Hands are tied because He will not violate our free will. In my opinion, this is like someone crying out with hunger but rejecting the food given to satiate the hunger pangs. Now, getting that out of the way, let us get back to the 'Four For One' Spiritual Gold.

If we use the opposite of love, the hormones have the opposite effect. Therefore, we must know or have an idea of the opposite of whatever actions, reactions, thoughts, or words that we are using or engaging in. For example, the opposite of love is hate. When exhibiting hate, it pumps the brakes on the 'Four For One' good hormones, releasing the harmful ones.

When exhibiting kindness, one of the primary chemicals released is oxytocin, often referred to as the love or bonding hormone. This overlook or underestimated hormone promotes feelings of love, social bonding, and connection, fostering positive or negative interactions, influences, and relationships.

In addition, acts of kindness release another hormone called endorphins, which are neurotransmitters, acting as natural pain relievers and mood elevators to boost the inner man or tame the psyche. How so? Endorphins contribute to feelings of pleasure, a sense of happiness, and contentment when managed properly.

Believe it or not, acts of kindness have also been associated with the release of dopamine in the brain. When we engage in acts of kindness, such as helping others or being charitable, our brain may release dopamine, which is often referred to as a feel-good neurotransmitter, contributing to positive feelings and a sense of reward or accomplishment that we experience when we engage in acts of kindness. By Divine Design, it is one of the reasons why helping others can be such a rewarding, invigorating, and uplifting feeling.

And then, we have serotonin, a neurotransmitter associated with feelings of happiness and well-being. Serotonin is also released when we engage in acts of kindness, regulating our moods, sleep patterns, relaxing tendencies, and appetites. All of which contribute to an overall sense of positivity and satisfaction of TOGETHERNESS. Ecclesiastes 4:9-10 says, *"Two are better than one, because they have a good reward for their labor. For if they fall, one will lift up his companion. But woe to him who is alone when he falls, for he has no one to help him up."*

When all 'Four For One' iron sharpening iron hormones (oxytocin, endorphins, dopamine, and serotonin) are used, *As It Pleases God*, through our selfless acts of kindness, they bring Spiritual Equilibrium to our 'Power Four' (Mind, Body, Soul, and Spirit), making us Powerful. Even amid chaos, confusion, or disarray, kindness places a Spiritual Seal on Proverbs 27:17: *"As iron sharpens iron, so a man sharpens the countenance of his friend."*

How do we make kindness make sense in the real world? Kindness is an ACTIONABLE TRAIT derived from love. Actually, it is our moral obligation, and it keeps us humble in the Eye of God and before mankind. *"Love suffers long and is kind; love does not envy; love does not parade itself, is not puffed up."* 1 Corinthians 13:4.

Kindness is one of the most avoided Spiritual Fruits in the Basket of Greatness. Why do we avoid being kind? It makes us appear weak to the predatorial vultures looking for fresh meat or someone to use or bully. Not realizing that Ephesians 4:32 says, *"And be kind to one another, tenderhearted, forgiving one another, even as God in Christ forgave you."*

Nonetheless, if we selflessly use kindness, *As It Pleases God*, instead of the vultures getting meat, they get MEEKNESS instead, with a recompensable agenda (GREAT REWARD) attached on our behalf. Really? Yes. Really!

In the Kindness Inspection, here are the prerequisites of God's Chosen Elect according to Colossians 3:12-15: *"Therefore, as the elect of God, holy and beloved, put on tender mercies, kindness, humility, meekness, longsuffering; bearing with one another, and forgiving one another, if anyone has a complaint against another; even as Christ forgave you, so you also must do. But above all these things put on love, which is the bond of perfection. And let the peace of God rule in your hearts, to which also you were called in one body; and be thankful."*

What if we opt not to be kind? We have free will to become selfishly unkind. Kindness is not a forced commodity. However, unkindness, hatefulness, unforgiveness, and unresolved anger come with their own set of repercussions, with the release of hormones such as adrenaline and cortisol.

Unfortunately, the hormonal release of adrenaline and cortisol is part of the body's natural stress hormone response to perceived threats, dangers, and psychological stressors. This stressor is often referred to as the fight-or-flight response that no one is exempt from. According to the Heavenly of Heavens, we are not designed to remain in this state of being 24/7. We must master the ability to turn it off to avoid making quick, rash, or unwarranted decisions. Turning the negative flow of emotions off helps to avoid engaging in indecisive actions in unfavorable, unwarranted, or challenging situations.

Let us talk about these two hormones for a moment. Here is the deal: Adrenaline increases the heart rate and blood pressure, providing a burst of energy. In contrast, cortisol is released in response to stress. It can have widespread effects on the body, including increasing blood sugar levels, suppressing the immune system, mobilizing energy reserves, regulating metabolism, influencing our immune functions, and swaying the body's response to stress.

While we do not often pay attention to them, these hormonal responses are part of the body's adaptive mechanisms designed to prepare us for perceived threats or challenges. However, prolonged or intense release of these hormones can have negative effects, Mentally, Physically, Emotionally, and Spiritually, especially when crying wolf, being the big bad wolf, or a wolf in sheep's clothing.

All in all, we must prepare the body for action and cope with these stressors by using the Fruits of the Spirit, *As It*

Pleases God. Why? Chronic stress and negative emotions, thoughts, beliefs, and speaking due to underlying unkindness, hatefulness, abusiveness, and anger prolong the elevation of cortisol and adrenaline levels.

Realistically, this can have long-term effects on the Power Four (Mind, Body, Soul, and Spirit), impacting the regulation of the 'Four For One' iron-sharpening-iron hormones (oxytocin, endorphins, dopamine, and serotonin). This loss causes us to become internally dysfunctional, powerless, and Kingdomly Unusable.

Why would we become unusable as Believers? First, it affects our cognitive functions, making us hot-tempered when we cannot control our negative emotions. Secondly, it affects our decision-making skills, attentiveness, obedience, and enthusiasm. Thirdly, it allows the psyche to harbor silent depression or oppression, making us emotional, sensitive, defensive, ungrateful, selfish, and easily triggerable. When we fail to use the common acts of kindness, do we think God will give us the Keys and Secrets to the Kingdom? No, He will not until we sort ourselves out, *As It Pleases Him!* Here is what Proverbs 11:17 says, *"The merciful man does good for his own soul, but he who is cruel troubles his own flesh."*

Before moving on to the Goodness Inspection, here is the Spiritual Seal for the kindness bonding factors that help us gain Kingdom Keys, Wisdom, and Secrets: *"But love your enemies, do good, and lend, hoping for nothing in return; and your reward will be great, and you will be sons of the Most High. For He is kind to the unthankful and evil."* Luke 6:35.

Goodness Inspection

Goodness is basically a practice of doing the right things, especially when having the opportunity to do wrong, pay someone back through retribution, get even with retaliation, be tempted to out someone by putting them on blast, or when the wrong things are happening to us.

In the face of adversity or any form of temptation, it is so easy to slip out of positive character to negative based on our thoughts, actions, reactions, words, beliefs, conditioning, mindsets, heart postures, and triggering traumas. We are faced with times when selfishness often takes precedence over selflessness, so here is the Goodness Rule: *"Therefore, whatever you want men to do to you, do also to them, for this is the Law and the Prophets."* Matthew 7:12.

In the Eye of God, the heart posture of goodness encourages generosity, empathy, trust, and moral excellence, creating transformativeness and powerfulness in the Kingdom. When goodness manifests itself in everyday actions automatically, we will know that we are working with a hot commodity from the Heavenly of Heavens.

Listen, there is some form of goodness hidden in everything. It is our responsibility to pinpoint the good or reverse bad to good through our thoughts, actions, reactions, words, or mindsets. For example, here are a few ways to express or become aware of goodness, but not limited to such:

- ☐ Pray for opportunities to be a BLESSING.
- ☐ Be kind to yourself and others.
- ☐ Smile often.
- ☐ Compliment others.
- ☐ Hold the door open for someone.
- ☐ Be respectful and courteous.
- ☐ Spread positivity.
- ☐ Be inclusive.
- ☐ Be understanding.
- ☐ Be patient with yourself and others.
- ☐ Check on those who appreciate kind gestures.
- ☐ Offer a sincere compliment.
- ☐ Listen attentively to others.

- ☐ Volunteer for something.
- ☐ Offer a helping hand to someone in need.
- ☐ Donate.
- ☐ Say 'please' and 'thank you' often.
- ☐ Offer your seat to someone in need.
- ☐ Send a thoughtful text or message.
- ☐ Offer to help a coworker with a task.
- ☐ Share a meal.
- ☐ Offer words of encouragement.
- ☐ Be patient and understanding.
- ☐ Give someone a genuine hug.
- ☐ Share your knowledge and skills with others.
- ☐ Practice empathy and compassion.
- ☐ Show appreciation and gratefulness.

Why must we go through the changes and jump through hoops to find the elements of goodness? There are lessons attached to them, like pots of gold or diamonds in the rough that are PREDESTINELY God-Made, not manmade. They are uniquely hidden for us according to our Predestined Blueprint, like manna falling from Heaven.

In our *Spirit to Spirit* Communion with our Heavenly Father, if we are stumped on finding the hidden elements of goodness, all we need to do is ask, 'What is it?' Then, document the answer! Why document? Goodness is always hidden in the documentation when putting pen to paper while reciting: "*My heart is overflowing with a good theme; I recite my composition concerning the King; My tongue is the pen of a ready writer.*" Psalm 45:1.

When sowing seeds of goodness, we can trust that God has our backs regardless of how it appears to the naked eye. What if we do not know how to sow good seeds? Ask God for help by repeating this: "*You are good, and do good; Teach me Your statutes.*" Psalm 119:68. Does this really work? Absolutely! James 1:17 says, "*Every good gift and every perfect gift is from above, and comes down from the Father of lights, with whom there is no variation or shadow of turning."*

Leading with authentic goodness can make goodness contagious, leaving a lasting impression on the hearts of those we encounter. Then again, it can also create a chain reaction of positive action as well. For example, several people can witness an accident, and once the first person begins to run toward the accident, stepping into action to help, it creates a chain reaction for the others to step up to the plate to help out as well. Why does this happen? Goodness is already built into our DNA; therefore, we cannot allow the gunk of life to clog our goodness pores. Here are a few examples of what clog our goodness pores, but not limited to such:

- ☐ Selfishness.
- ☐ Debauchery.
- ☐ Wickedness.
- ☐ Sinfulness.
- ☐ Lies.
- ☐ Immorality.
- ☐ Badness.
- ☐ Wrongdoing.
- ☐ Corruption.
- ☐ Depravity.
- ☐ Malice.
- ☐ Cruelty.
- ☐ Hatred.
- ☐ Spitefulness.
- ☐ Injustice.
- ☐ Dishonesty.
- ☐ Unkindness.
- ☐ Viciousness.
- ☐ Rudeness.

We can go on with this list for days...but you get the picture. The bottom line is that goodness is indeed a TESTAMENT to strength, faithfulness, and endurance from the inside out. And, when doing a Faithfulness Inspection, I will look for the simple acts of goodness. Why? It shows that we have the capacity to care for something or someone else outside of ourselves.

Faithfulness Inspection

Faithfulness is something we all have, even if we fail to use it, mismanage it, or are deprived of experiencing it with others. The bottom line is that we are all faithful to something. Right or wrong, good or bad, just or unjust, positive or negative, we are still exercising some form of faith. While doing our due diligence in where we place our faithfulness, we must know this: *"The integrity of the upright will guide them, but the perversity of the unfaithful will destroy them."* Proverbs 11:3.

In the Kingdom of God, the goal is to develop a faithful heart posture or stance using what we have in our hands, *As It Pleases Him* with upright integrity. Of course, no one is perfect, but we must try our best with a work-in-progress mindset.

For example, we would not just leave a building to rot; we would work on it daily for its upkeep. So, we are no different! Here is the ideal situation: *"His lord said to him, 'Well done, good and faithful servant; you were faithful over a few things, I will make you ruler over many things. Enter into the joy of your lord.'"* Matthew 25:23.

In the Eye of God, faithfulness represents trustworthiness, loyalty, and commitment to His Divine Will. Once we come into AGREEMENT with our Predestined Blueprint, it will sustain our hopefulness and our reason for being. Why do we need them? They will keep us from giving up easily!

Although we do not want to associate faithfulness outside of God, then again, as Believers, we want to bogart it, making faithfulness sacredly our own. Understandably so, the truth is faithfulness is for everyone, the good, bad, or indifferent, making it work for us or against us.

Here is the deal on faithfulness: We exhibit faithfulness in the Kingdom of God and outside of it. Both are demonstrations of our commitment to places where we have established loyalty and value. Regardless of where we encounter it on the journey, it does not negate its power or its uses when applied properly to all aspects of our lives.

For example, the non-believers are hell-bent on discrediting the Believers. Meanwhile, Believers are hell-bent on taking down the non-believers coming against them. They both are faithful in their method of operation, so the question is, 'Who is the winner in the faithfulness battle?' Do we even know? It is the one with the best character or the best heart posture, *As It Pleases God*. Blasphemy, right? Wrong!

We can debate for days about who is right or wrong about the appropriation of faithfulness. Nevertheless, in the Fruit Inspection process, according to Galatians 5:22-23, Paul writes that there is no law against the Fruits of the Spirit. In all simplicity, we are operating with Spiritual Laws against everything else concerning our faithfulness, except for the use of the Fruits of the Spirit.

Why is there no need for a law to regulate or restrict the Fruits of the Spirit? The proper use of the Spiritual Fruits makes our character Christlike, *As It Pleases God*. All of which will naturally align us with His Divine Will, our Predestined Blueprint, and the Spiritual Provisions needed to get us to where we need to be.

Ephesians 5:9 says, *"For the fruit of the Spirit is in all goodness, righteousness, and truth."* Therefore, in our faithfulness, when weighing one against the other, we must ask these three questions:

☐ In our faithfulness, are we operating in goodness?

- ☐ In our faithfulness, are we operating in righteousness?
- ☐ In our faithfulness, are we operating in truth?

Why must we ask ourselves these three questions concerning our faithfulness? In the Faithfulness Inspection, they will determine if we walk in LOVE, walk in LIGHT, and walk in WISDOM. Conversely, they will also determine if we walk in hatefulness, walk in darkness, and walk in foolery.

In our Faithfulness Inspection, when the INDWELLING of the Holy Spirit guides us, it makes the contending factors of our faithfulness supersede those with whom He does not guide, provide, or abide. *"I say then: Walk in the Spirit, and you shall not fulfill the lust of the flesh."* Galatians 5:16.

Without this level of faithfulness or the Indwelling of the Holy Spirit, we revert to what we are working with from a worldly perspective. Still, there are no Spiritual Guarantees when we place our faithfulness in the secular.

What is the secular? Unfortunately, this is when we place our faithfulness and focus on material gain, success, wealth, status, power, selfishness, independence, and instant gratification, which often seems to contradict Spiritual Values and Principles according to the Heavenly of Heavens. Here is what happens when we avoid doing what we were called to do to embrace secular faithfulness instead, but not limited to such:

- ☐ It leads to inner conflict.
- ☐ It leads to insecurities.
- ☐ It leads to a sense of being unfulfilled.
- ☐ It leads to a sense of emptiness.
- ☐ It leads to disillusionment.
- ☐ It leads to confusion.
- ☐ It leads to fleeting desires.
- ☐ It leads to being unsatisfied.

- ☐ It leads to yearning for something more.
- ☐ It leads to setting false expectations.
- ☐ It leads to feeling adrift.
- ☐ It leads to stunted growth.
- ☐ It leads to feeling disconnected.
- ☐ It leads to becoming extremely judgmental.

Now, the question is, 'Can we exhibit faithfulness and unfaithfulness simultaneously?' Absolutely! Dualism will always exist. So, wherever there is faithfulness, the opposite will be evident! *"For what if some did not believe? Will their unbelief make the faithfulness of God without effect?"* Romans 3:3.

Nevertheless, within dualism in our Fruit Inspection process, we decide these factors of right or wrong, good or bad, just or unjust, positive or negative, and faithfulness or unfaithfulness by our thoughts, actions, reactions, words, biases, desires, fruits, traumas, mindsets, and decisions. Here are a few ways to build faithfulness, but not limited to such:

- ☐ Spend time in prayer daily.
- ☐ Communicate with God, *Spirit to Spirit*.
- ☐ We must seek the guidance of the Holy Spirit.
- ☐ Cover ourselves with the Blood of Jesus for Atonement.
- ☐ Study the Word of God.
- ☐ Meditate on the teachings of the Bible.
- ☐ Understand God's Divine Will and Ways.
- ☐ Understand our Predestined Blueprinted Mission.
- ☐ Attend church services regularly to worship.
- ☐ Fellowship or assemble with other believers.
- ☐ Serve others with love and compassion.
- ☐ Use the Fruits of the Spirit.
- ☐ Behave Christlike.
- ☐ Live by example.
- ☐ Trust in God's promises.

- ☐ Live a life of integrity and honesty.
- ☐ Be authentically truthful.
- ☐ Reflects God's love, grace, and mercy.
- ☐ Practice forgiveness and reconciliation.
- ☐ Be obedient to God's commandments.
- ☐ Live a life that honors God, *As It Pleases Him*.
- ☐ Share the message of God's love and salvation.
- ☐ Choose words, deeds, and actions carefully.
- ☐ Practice humility.
- ☐ Practice gratitude and thanksgiving in all things.
- ☐ Understand we are Blessed to be a Blessing.
- ☐ Live with moral uprightness.
- ☐ Share with others unselfishly.
- ☐ Seek wisdom and guidance from God, *As It Pleases Him*.
- ☐ Trust in God's Divine Provision.
- ☐ Practice patience and perseverance.
- ☐ Understand that God's timing is perfect.
- ☐ Remain positive.
- ☐ Pinpoint the win-win.
- ☐ Continue learning, growing, and becoming, *As It Pleases God*.

All of which leads to gaining the wisdom, courage, and hope needed to Grow Great, *As It Pleases God*.

Now, regardless of how we view faithfulness or how we use it, we must realize that God is faithful to us, even amid our falling short. In the Eye of God, here is what we should do: *"Trust in the LORD, and do good; Dwell in the land, and feed on His faithfulness. Delight yourself also in the LORD, And He shall give you the desires of your heart. Commit your way to the LORD, Trust also in Him, And He shall bring it to pass."* Psalm 37:3-5.

Gentleness Inspection

Gentleness is required of us in the Eye of God. Why? The power of being gentle as Believers promotes sensitivity, softness, humility, meekness, and compassion. All of these are conveyed through our words, touch, approach, thoughts, actions, reactions, biases, desires, fruits, traumas, mindsets, and decisions. Even if we do not understand them, it does not void the positive or negative effects associated.

How can gentleness possibly affect our Spiritual Relationship with our Heavenly Father? Believe it or not, the way we speak, all the way to how we behave, matters to God. Why does it matter? We represent Him and the Kingdom. Plus, we also have Spiritual Etiquette hanging in the balance to determine the notches on our belt or whether chastisement is needed.

When operating in the Boldness of God, we often associate doing so with strength, assertiveness, and courage, causing the characteristics of gentleness to get lost in the shuffle. Proverbs 24:5 clearly says, *"A wise man is strong, yes, a man of knowledge increases strength."* Simply put, we must gain knowledge to increase the inner man properly. Why? Our strength is not a standalone commodity in the Kingdom. There are underlying factors contributing to our WHY.

Meanwhile, in the pursuit of understanding ourselves or refusing to do so, what is expected of us becomes overlooked by the frugality of living life with a thwarted preconceived image of the Mind or Ways of God.

According to the Heavenly of Heavens, gentleness and humility have more COMEBACK and COMBAT power than the rod of toughness and pompousness. How is this humanly possible, especially when people take our gentleness as a weakness? In the Eye of God, gentleness is not a weakness; it is a hidden, quiet strength that comes from a place of confidence and trust. Whereas, on the other hand, toughness and pompousness are derived from insecurities, the lack of confidence, and the absence of trust.

Once again, gentleness allows us to navigate our words, touch, approach, thoughts, actions, reactions, biases, desires, fruits, traumas, mindsets, and decisions with grace and compassion. The absence of it will be conveyed in the navigational process of what we do, say, become, and the lack thereof.

For the sake of gentleness, this is what 2 Timothy 2:24-26 shares with us: *"And a servant of the Lord must not quarrel but be gentle to all, able to teach, patient, in humility correcting those who are in opposition, if God perhaps will grant them repentance, so that they may know the truth, and that they may come to their senses and escape the snare of the devil, having been taken captive by him to do his will."* Here are a few ways to extend gentleness, but not limited to such:

- ☐ Practice active listening when someone is speaking.
- ☐ Use a calm and soothing tone of voice.
- ☐ Offer words of encouragement.
- ☐ Be supportive and helpful.
- ☐ Show empathy towards others' feelings.
- ☐ Relate to the experiences of others.
- ☐ Be patient.
- ☐ Be understanding in challenging situations.
- ☐ Handle delicate objects with care.
- ☐ Exhibit a caring demeanor.
- ☐ Avoid using harsh language.
- ☐ Avoid making hurtful remarks.
- ☐ Offer a comforting hug.
- ☐ Use kind gestures.
- ☐ Be mindful of personal space.
- ☐ Avoid violating boundaries.
- ☐ Help others without expecting anything in return.
- ☐ Speak kindly to yourself and others.

- ☐ Practice self-compassion.
- ☐ Approach conflicts.
- ☐ Seek peaceful resolutions.
- ☐ Show appreciation.
- ☐ Express emotions gently and respectfully.
- ☐ Be considerate of others' perspectives.
- ☐ Respect the feelings of others.
- ☐ Apologize, forgive, and repent quickly.
- ☐ Offer assistance to those in need.
- ☐ Use gentle and nurturing touch when appropriate.
- ☐ Extend understanding regarding mistakes.
- ☐ Treat animals with care.
- ☐ Be respectful and kind to nature.
- ☐ Practice gentleness in thoughts, words, and actions.

In all reality, gentleness is a powerful and transformative quality that can enrich our lives and the lives of those around us. It involves a conscious effort to approach others and ourselves with kindness, empathy, and understanding.

Self-Control Inspection

Self-control is what we all have hidden within the depths of our souls, yet we often do not take the time to use it. Due to the lack of understanding of how it works, *As It Pleases God*. Self-control is a self-preserving mechanism hidden within the conscience, helping us to navigate through the dualism we face with our Heaven on Earth Experiences.

For example, when we lose control or zone out, we must first violate our conscience and do whatever it is anyway. The more this violation occurs, the more out of control we become, allowing the psyche to run the show based on our feelings and not our Spiritual Faculties designed to safeguard, alert, and protect us through our recognizable senses.

More importantly, self-control is the final fruit mentioned, emphasizing the importance of mastering one's desires and impulses to sustain our Spiritual Fruits.

Self-control is a GIFT with a Spiritual Compass (the conscience) that was given to mankind based on the Garden of Eden debacle with Adam and Eve. It allows us the free will to exercise discipline, restraint, and temperance to avoid provoking the Wrath of God. In addition, it also assists in avoiding bringing shame to our names by helping us to govern ourselves, to resist temptations, and to make choices that align with our values, integrity, and beliefs, *As It Pleases God.*

Above all, according to Galatians 5:22-23, there is no law against using self-control in the commission of using the Fruits of the Spirit. However, FAILING to use self-control nullifies the 'NO LAW' Spiritual Clause, invoking the relevant Spiritual Laws and Principles associated with whatever, wherever, however, whyever, and with whomever. Is this fair? Absolutely! In my opinion, it is similar to the Use It or Lose It cliché.

Without self-control, denying oneself of indulgences or pleasures, we will accrue a track record of continual wrath, shame, blame, disdain, and division. All of these are associated with negative thoughts, selfishness, impulsive behaviors, harmful habits, debauchery, distractions, temptations, instant gratification, and destructive patterns that lead us away from a life of righteousness, oneness, and holiness.

Just keep in mind that anything associated with the lust of the eyes, the lust of the flesh, and the pride of life contains a Spiritual Yoke. Why would this happen, especially when having free will? Disobedience causes us to become Spiritually Deaf, Blind, and Mute to our Heavenly Father and our Predestined Blueprint, even if we think we have it going on.

How can we make self-control work for us? One will need humility, obedience, discipline, restraint, and *"Be anxious for nothing, but in everything by prayer and supplication, with thanksgiving, let your requests be made known to God; and the peace of God, which surpasses all understanding, will guard your hearts and minds through Christ Jesus."* Philippians 4:6-7. Here are a few ways to develop self-control, but not limited to such:

- ☐ Place the Holy Trinity first.
- ☐ Add God into the equation of all things.
- ☐ Cover yourself with the Blood of Jesus.
- ☐ Request guidance from the Holy Spirit.
- ☐ Test the Spirit.
- ☐ Seek wisdom in the matter.
- ☐ Meditate on the Word of God.
- ☐ Set specific, achievable goals.
- ☐ Exercise delayed gratification.
- ☐ Manage stress effectively.
- ☐ Learn to say no!
- ☐ Use the Fruits of the Spirit.
- ☐ Practice self-reflection and correction.
- ☐ Seek support and accountability.
- ☐ Limit exposure to temptations.
- ☐ Practice self-discipline in small ways.
- ☐ Use positive self-talk.
- ☐ Develop a growth mindset.
- ☐ Identify and avoid triggers.
- ☐ Improve problem-solving skills.
- ☐ Set boundaries.
- ☐ Encourage yourself.
- ☐ Learn to manage impulses.
- ☐ Cultivate patience and peacefulness.
- ☐ Celebrate small victories.

Now, if you think you can exhibit total self-control without God, then have at it. But let me say this: Self-control works best with the ONE who created it for our sake, with a transformative power that transcends earthly laws, regulations, human psychology, and mind games. More importantly, know this: *"He who follows righteousness and mercy finds life, righteousness, and honor."* Proverbs 21:21.

The Use of Spiritual Fruits

We must USE the Fruits of the Spirit in order for them to become Spiritually Effective, molding our character from worldly to Christlike to walk in the LIGHT. *"For you were once darkness, but now you are light in the Lord. For the fruit of the Spirit is in all goodness, righteousness, and truth, finding out what is acceptable to the Lord."* Ephesians 5:8-10.

Why must we exhibit good fruits when encountering rotten fruits? Our fruits are not for our selfish consumption. Our fruits are for us to develop and share with others, to Divinely Protect us from them, or to prevent them from gaining leverage to sucker-punch us with things that God dislikes.

For example, if you desire love, give it. If you want joy, give it. If you want peace, give it. If you desire kindness, give it. If you want goodness, give it. If you want faithfulness, give it. If you desire gentleness, give it. If you desire self-control, give it. Once again, once it is given as a free-will offering, we will draw these fruits or character traits back to us in due season based upon the Law of Reciprocity or Seedtime and Harvest. Plus, we get to enjoy the hormonal release of oxytocin, endorphins, dopamine, and serotonin, and the lowering of our cortisol benefits instantly.

If our fruits are not leading the way toward the hormonal benefits, then they could be a part of the problem. Therefore, *"Have no fellowship with the unfruitful works of darkness, but rather expose them."* Ephesians 5:11. To be clear, this does not mean to put people on blast! We must live by example, and all we need to do is say, 'No, thank you' to bad fruits, character traits, words, thoughts, beliefs, ideologies, and so on.

On the other hand, prayer, repentance, forgiveness, meditation, mercy, and our *Spirit to Spirit* Relations with our Heavenly Father are indeed for us. Then again, it is for our purity and sanity, or helping our Fruits of the Spirit tame the traumatizations or quirks of the psyche, getting to the root of matters. James 3:17-18 nails it when it says: *"But the wisdom that is from above is first pure, then peaceable, gentle, willing to yield, full of mercy and good fruits, without partiality and without hypocrisy. Now the fruit of righteousness is sown in peace by those who make peace."*

For example, you will never see a tree consuming its own fruits; it is for the lifecycle of others, while using what is NOT consumed as fertilizer (preparation) for the next batch. Matthew 7:16-18 says, *"You will know them by their fruits. Do men gather grapes from thornbushes or figs from thistles? Even so, every good tree bears good fruit, but a bad tree bears bad fruit. A good tree cannot bear bad fruit, nor can a bad tree bear good fruit."*

How do we break this negative cycle and avoid consuming our own fruits? To become a new man, *As It Pleases God*, Colossians 3:5-8 says, *"Therefore put to death your members which are on the earth: fornication, uncleanness, passion, evil desire, and covetousness, which is idolatry. Because of these things the wrath of God is coming upon the sons of disobedience, in which you yourselves once walked when you lived in them. But now you yourselves are to put off all these: anger, wrath, malice, blasphemy, filthy language out of your mouth."*

What if we choose not to become new, *As It Pleases God*? We have free will to remain the same, but we must respect another man's territory, period! Why? Bogarting or bullying with or without incorporating the Holy Spirit is a big Spiritual No-No. If we opt out of bringing newness into our own lives, we should not hinder others from exercising their free will to accept the newness Jesus offered to all of us on the CROSS.

Why is bogarting and bullying disliked in the Eye of God? The Holy Spirit will lie dormant at the drop of a dime, pumping the brakes on whatever or whomever. Here is what Proverbs 6:16-19 says, *"There are six things the Lord hates, seven that are detestable to him: haughty eyes, a lying tongue, hands that shed innocent blood, a heart that devises wicked schemes, feet that are quick to rush into evil, a false witness who pours out lies and a person who stirs up conflict in the community."*

Nevertheless, with all due respect, bullying or intimidating others does not make it right, effective, or conducive to our Spiritual Well-being or *As It Pleases God*. What if we are on the receiving end of this? The enemy does not know where our heads or weaknesses are until we open our mouths. So, the moment we open it, we had better make sure that it is not a weapon that can be used against us and that we have done our homework thoroughly.

Why is thoroughness required from Believers? Recklessness is not a characteristic that the Kingdom will trust with Divine Wisdom, Secrets, and Treasures.

To be clear, we all make mistakes; however, self-correcting and deflecting determine the usable, trainable, disobedient, stiff-necked, dullness, or remedial. Although no one is perfect, we must also understand that no one is exempt from negativity or negative character traits. However, we all have the potential to become a work-in-progress, trying to become better, stronger, and wiser, *As It Pleases God*.

Amid the Fruit Inspection, know this: *"Blessed is the man who walks not in the counsel of the ungodly, nor stands in the path of sinners, nor sits in the seat of the scornful; But his delight is in the law of the Lord, And in His law he meditates day and night. He shall be like a tree planted by the rivers of water, that brings forth its fruit in its season, whose leaf also shall not wither; And whatever he does shall prosper."* Psalm 1:1-3.

More importantly, do not feel bad when rejecting negative fruits. It is your God-Given Spiritual Right of dualism to make sure that your Tree of Life remains, *As It Pleases Him*. Plus, you have the Fruits of the Spirit as a guideline to what is expected of you. So, you do not have to walk around pulling for straws or plugging and playing...the Spiritual Roadmap is already provided for you, and it is your responsibility to use it for your Spiritual Journey.

How do we make the dualism of our Spiritual Rights make sense on our Spiritual Journey? Let us understand the Spiritual Seal associated with dualism and Spiritually TILLING your own ground. *"Then the LORD God said, 'Behold, the man has become like one of Us, to know good and evil. And now, lest he put out his hand and take also of the tree of life, and eat, and live forever'—therefore the LORD God sent him out of the garden of Eden to till the ground from which he was taken."* Genesis 3:22-23.

Here is the deal: Whether you understand the Divine Process metaphorically or realistically, the Tree of Life is within you, containing soil, roots, seeds, branches, thorns, leaves, and fruits. In reality, all of these equate to your words, thoughts, beliefs, biases, desires, actions, reactions, attitudes, characteristics, experiences, and traumas.

Before moving on to the Work-In-Progress Mentality, you are held accountable for developing, maintaining, and harvesting your Spiritual Fruits, ensuring they do not cause you to become a Tree of Death.

More importantly, you are accountable for allowing someone to taint your fruits as well. Romans 14:12 says, *"So then each of us shall give account of himself to God."* And, *"For each one shall bear his own load."* Galatians 6:5. *"But the fruit of the righteous is a tree of life, And he who wins souls is wise."* Proverbs 11:30. So, let us get to work!

How do we win souls to the Kingdom with our Spiritual Fruits? Here are a few tips, but not limited to such:

☐ Live a life that reflects the love of Jesus Christ.

- ☐ Behave Christlike.
- ☐ Use the Fruits of the Spirit.
- ☐ Share your personal Testimony.
- ☐ Share your faith with others.
- ☐ Pray for others.
- ☐ Engage in meaningful and positive conversations.
- ☐ Show kindness and compassion to those in need.
- ☐ Invite people to church or Christian events.
- ☐ Use social media to share inspirational messages.
- ☐ Share Bible verses.
- ☐ Volunteer for community service projects.
- ☐ Host a Bible study or prayer group in your home.
- ☐ Be a good listener.
- ☐ Ask good fact-finding questions.
- ☐ Support those who are struggling.
- ☐ Organize or participate in mission trips.
- ☐ Be open and available to answer questions.
- ☐ Encourage others to seek a relationship with God.
- ☐ Use your talents and skills to serve others.
- ☐ Glorify God in your words, thoughts, and beliefs.
- ☐ Be patient and understanding.
- ☐ Build genuine relationships of trust.
- ☐ Demonstrate joy and peace.
- ☐ Trust in the power of the Holy Spirit for guidance.

Using this checklist will help you stay focused on doing Kingdom Business, *As It Pleases God*.

CHAPTER 9

Work-In-Progress Mentality

The Work-In-Progress Mentality is here to stay! In or out of the Kingdom of God, this mindset is a refreshing and empowering alternative way to grow and develop on our continuous journey through life, *As It Pleases God*. Equally important, this mindset helps us to understand setbacks, mistakes, and challenges from a Divine Perspective, leaving no viable stone unturned.

Overcoming the fear of stepping out of our comfort zones is something we will all face at some point in our lives. Frankly, it is the challenges that push us into our next seasons, right? The Vicissitudes and Cycles of Life are designed to put us to work with ourselves or on ourselves to facilitate the pruning process of dead or hindering weight. In my opinion, this is similar to how the body sheds dead skin cells; we cannot usually see how it is done, but it successfully does its job with or without our permission.

Once we begin to build momentum, here are a few items that we can glean from developing a Work-In-Progress Mentality, *As It Pleases God*, but not limited to such:

- ☐ We can unlock our full potential.
- ☐ We can confront our limitations.
- ☐ We can become open to new experiences.
- ☐ We can embrace change with a positive mindset.
- ☐ We can create a win-win out of an apparent lose-lose.

- ☐ We will view obstacles as opportunities.
- ☐ We can excel in learning, developing, and pruning.
- ☐ We will master the regrafting process.
- ☐ We can foster a sense of resilience and adaptability.
- ☐ We can focus on ongoing self-improvement.
- ☐ We can master self-correction or self-analysis.
- ☐ We can embrace a proactive approach.
- ☐ We can think on our feet or at the drop of a dime.
- ☐ We will be able to seek and accept feedback.
- ☐ We will know how to bounce back from failures.
- ☐ We will understand that our setbacks are setups.
- ☐ We can embrace the power of our Creative Minds.
- ☐ We can develop and master a proactive approach.

The Work-In-Progress Mentality helps us accept ourselves for who we are and our imperfections while seeing them as a Diamond in the Rough. Why? It motivates us to work on them, grow through them, and share them by activating the Law of Reciprocity to BLESS the works of our hands. *"If the axe is dull, and one does not sharpen the edge, then he must use more strength; but wisdom brings success."* Ecclesiastes 10:10. Although some may not accept this concept; however, when it comes to dealing with Divine Purpose, *As It Pleases God*, we must continue to become better, stronger, and wiser.

What is the purpose of becoming a work-in-progress, especially when no one is perfect? Doing something, doing nothing, or lying about our condition means everything regarding our Creative Mindset or the restrictions imposed.

Why would we become restricted from having a Creative Mindset? We can become really deceptive or manipulative while appearing right in our own eyes. Although we are not barred from worldly creativity, we are restricted from the Divine Creativity of the Kingdom due to the probable misuse based on the Garden of Eden Experience. Here is what James

1:26 says, "*If anyone among you thinks he is religious, and does not bridle his tongue but deceives his own heart, this one's religion is useless.*"

For me, the moment someone opens their mouth, it will confirm everything I already know about them. Simply put, when TESTING the Spirit or asking, 'Who sent you?' as I am required to do, if their words or fruits do not confirm, it is considered speculation in the natural and Spiritual Realm.

In reality, this is similar to having a thought about something or someone, and if we do not put any ACTIONS or WORDS behind the thought, it will remain just that, a thought. So, "*He who guards his mouth preserves his life, but he who opens wide his lips shall have destruction.*" Proverbs 13:3. For this reason, it is only wise to learn a little more about our Words in Progress according to Kingdom Standards and how we are Divinely Created.

Words in Progress

The words we use are verbal exchanges of triggers in the earthly realm and the Heavenly Realm alike, making us wordfully trigger happy or sad. The formulation of words is a GIFT to mankind, and they are not meant for us to make a word salad of debauchery to appear superior to the next man.

Our audible spoken language should not be taken for granted, nor should we misuse it for our benefit, to blasphemingly mock another, or disable another selfishly, even if we feel justified in doing so, or we get a little chuckle from the backfire of the onset of folly. Clearly, this does not mean we cannot respond, stand up for ourselves, or speak the truth in love. It is learning HOW to respond or stand our ground, *As It Pleases God*, without fussing, fighting, or disrupting the flow of order. When operating decent and in order, *As It Pleases Him*, it sets us apart from the naysayers, player haters, or agitators.

To the core of our being, words are our power play or kryptonite. In all simplicity, words are triggers used to either uplift or tear down people, places, and things. Proverbs 15:7 says, *"The lips of the wise disperse knowledge, but the heart of the fool does not do so."*

In the Eye of God, what we disperse from our mouths gives us a bird's eye view of who we are and what we are about. Really? Yes, really! The words we use or what we hear can trigger hormones within the human body, positively or negatively. Our Heavenly Father is so strategic that even the natural sounds of nature, animals, and music affect us as well. Therefore, we must be careful about the positive and negative effects associated with what we set in motion by what comes out of our mouths.

For example, words with expressions of love, gratitude, and encouragement stimulate the release of oxytocin, often referred to as the love or bonding hormone. In addition, positive and affirming words release serotonin and dopamine, known as the feel-good neurotransmitters, to regulate our moods and emotional responses, lowering our cortisol. By Divine Design, they contribute to a sense of happiness, satisfaction, contentment, and emotional well-being.

On the other side of the coin, the detrimental effects of negative words, stressful chatter, harsh words, criticism, or degrading self-talk increase cortisol, stressing us out and causing anxiety, fear, chaos, stress, and panic. For sure, this is why the Bible says, *"A soft answer turns away wrath, but a harsh word stirs up anger."* Proverbs 15:1.

Prolonged exposure to negativity or harsh communication can lead to impaired immune functions, heightened risk of various health conditions, and trauma to the psyche. The truth of the matter is that we can feel the release of these hormones, especially when getting angry, frustrated, or having googly eyes for someone. But we do not know what they are, what they are associated with, or how they will impact us in the long run. Proverbs 19:2 says, "*Also it is not good for a soul to be without knowledge, and he sins who hastens with his feet.*"

We often want to run to the doctor when someone stresses us out or when we are out of control. Still, we often do not take the time to evaluate what is coming out of our mouths. Why should we check our mouthpieces first? Initially, stress does not originate from around us; it is derived from what is within us, spreading outwardly.

For example, we can have ten people experience the same situation, and we will get ten different responses. Let me explain: Before anything manifests in the physical, it has an internal Spiritual Component attached, such as soil, roots, seeds, branches, thorns, leaves, and fruits. Based on these components, it will determine our level of stress, responses, reactions, and resolves. Most often, it is our words, self-talk, inner chatter, disobedience, or rebellion that is making the psyche sick or placing us in a tailspin, Mentally, Physically, Emotionally, and Spiritually. Once again, this is why Proverbs 4:23 says, "*Keep your heart with all diligence, for out of it spring the issues of life.*"

According to the Ancient of Days, our words are designed to edify us and others; if they are not doing so, they will turn against us. Is this Biblical? I would have it no other way. "*The lips of the righteous feed many, but fools die for lack of wisdom.*" Proverbs 10:21. "*The fear of the Lord is the beginning of knowledge, but fools despise wisdom and instruction.*" Proverbs 1:7.

Here is the deal: Gentleness in speech involves speaking kindly, using soft words, and being mindful of how our words may affect others. The Divine Instructions from Colossians 4:6 are: "*Let your speech always be with grace, seasoned with salt, that you may know how you ought to answer each one.*"

Why must we season our words, especially when we want to let them have it? What will it solve or accomplish by letting them have it or letting them see that we lack self-control?

Here is what Ephesians 4:29 says, "*Let no corrupt word proceed out of your mouth, but what is good for necessary edification, that it may impart grace to the hearers.*"

We often hear that it is not what we say; it is how we say it, right? Then again, with all due respect, if one's vocabulary is limited, it is time to expand it to choose soft, kind, and palatable words. Even Google can tell us how to soften words. What if we do not have time to do so? Then, we should pray for the Holy Spirit to set a guard over our mouths. Does it work? Absolutely. However, we do not want to use this as a crutch...we must become a Work-In-Progress, making our best attempts to govern our words accordingly to keep hope alive. Proverbs 29:20 says, "*Do you see a man hasty in his words? There is more hope for a fool than for him.*"

Keep in mind that gentle words can soothe a troubled heart and mind and diffuse tense conversations and situations, especially when combined with the power of connection or touch. For example, we hear this all the time, 'Your words touched me.' How can our words touch without physically touching? It is the hormonal touch that gives our words power. Conversely, the same applies to using words to destroy, cast ill will, or cause harm, Mentally, Physically, Emotionally, or Spiritually.

So, with the Work-In-Progress Mentality, we are required to give thought to what comes out of our mouths. Proverbs 15:4 says, "*A wholesome tongue is a tree of life, but perverseness in it breaks the spirit.*"

Touch of Progress

Can touch really progress us? Can progression become recognized by how we touch people, places, and things? The answer is yes! Yes, to touch. Yes, to progress. Yes, to the Touch of Progress.

Here is the dealio of the Touch of Progress: Physical touch conveys attentiveness, care, comfort, and empathy, playing a crucial role in our social and emotional development. It is important to note that the power of touch affects our well-being, interpersonal relationships, bonding process, and connecting factors of rapport.

Unbeknown to most, the key hormone influenced by touch is oxytocin. Once again, it is often referred to as the love or bonding hormone. In addition to oxytocin, touch also influences the release of serotonin and dopamine in the same way that our words do.

These feel-good neurotransmitters are still associated with pleasure and reward, lowering the release of cortisol, the stress hormone. So, if we use the power of touch with kind words, we get a double portion of this Divine Goodness flowing through our people skills on our behalf and the receiver's behalf as well.

What if they do not receive the release of hormones? Our responsibility is to set them in motion selflessly, *As It Pleases God*. And, if they reject the impartation or the fruits, they have free will to do so because this can work both positively and negatively.

For example, if I get an inclination of negative vibes from something or someone, I am going to reject it, period! Why? My mindset is Spiritually Set on positive vibes only. Therefore, when my Spiritual Compass shifts, it is my responsibility to regulate it without violating my conscience or integrity. Suppose a division occurs when I am wholeheartedly using the Fruits of the Spirit, behaving Christlike, and placing the Holy Spirit at the forefront of all things. In this case, Jude 1:19 says, *"These are sensual persons, who cause divisions, not having the Spirit."*

How do we make touch make sense in the Touch of Progress? Whether the touch is a comforting hand on the shoulder, a nod, a reassuring hug, cuddling, or a non-contact hand gesture, physical or nonverbal touch can communicate empathy, trust, support, warmth, and understanding. All of which creates a sense of calm connection, a sense of happiness, a response of satisfaction, a soothing impact, a welcomed reassurance, a sense of security, and a palatable attachment amid personal boundaries.

All in all, we must use the power of touch to unite as ONE. If unity is not there or division occurs, back up! In the same way that we have a touch to build us, in the dualism from the Garden of Eden and *As It Pleases God*, we also have a do not touch (The Forbidden Fruit) as well. *"Now I urge you, brethren, note those who cause divisions and offenses, contrary to the doctrine which you learned, and avoid them."* Romans 16:17.

Encroachments or Spiritual Violations are not what we are aiming for here. The goal is to unveil our Blueprinted Passion or Purpose that has its own set of Spiritual Provisions.

With the Creative Mindset, as a rule of thumb, do not force any piece of your puzzle into a groove that it is not designed to fit. Why? It is the wrong attachment; therefore, we must change our approach before reproach or the Rod of Correction occurs to unravel our knits.

Here is what we must know before moving on to the Approach to Progress: *"For I want you to know what a great conflict I have for you and those in Laodicea, and for as many as have not seen my face in the flesh, that their hearts may be encouraged, being knit together in love, and attaining to all riches of the full assurance of understanding, to the knowledge of the mystery of God, both of the Father and of Christ, in whom are hidden all the treasures of wisdom and knowledge."* Colossians 2:1-3.

So, if you want it, whatever it is or is not, then let us approach it, *As It Pleases God*.

Approach to Progress

A gentle approach in the Eye of God involves being considerate and compassionate, conveying respect, empathy, safety, comfort, and understanding in our interactions with Him, ourselves, and others.

Why is our approach to God, people, places, things, and ourselves important? First, it is a matter of respect. Secondly, it is about Divine Order or Instructions. Thirdly, it pertains to having an understanding of how God wants things to be or pan out. Not how we want them or think they should be. Nor does it mean we should approach life without having Him in the equation, especially when it is He who sent us here in the first place.

In the Approach to Progress, Ephesians 4:14-16 wants us to know: *"We should no longer be children, tossed to and fro and carried about with every wind of doctrine, by the trickery of men, in the cunning craftiness of deceitful plotting, but, speaking the truth in love, may grow up in all things into Him who is the head—Christ—from whom the whole body, joined and knit together by what every joint supplies, according to the effective working by which every part does its share, causes growth of the body for the edifying of itself in love."*

When moving with God at the forefront of our lives, we must approach situations with a peaceful, non-cunning, and non-confrontational demeanor, seeking understanding and resolution rather than conflict, harshness, judgment, and aggression.

More importantly, in fostering open communication and trust, the ideal approach is first to be mindful of our tone of voice. Secondly, being considerate of other people's feelings and receptive to their viewpoints. Thirdly, allowing them to have their own perspectives, running their own race of free will. And lastly, it allows us to express our thoughts, opinions, and concerns in a non-threatening manner. This strategic approach encourages freedom, collaboration, and problem-solving without witticisms.

If we have a negative or punning approach to people, places, and things, it can cause them to withdraw from us, get on the defensive side of things, and sometimes blame God for our actionable approach. What is the big deal, especially when we have free will to communicate and approach how we so desire? When people are not vibing with our words, they are not going to vibe with our touch or approach to whatever, whenever, however, wherever, and with whomever.

Why can people not just accept who we are? Once this question is voiced internally or externally, it is an indication that one is not accepting oneself. Unfortunately, having this lingering question hanging out in the psyche causes their vibes to become a nuisance. Meanwhile, they try to force others to accept their lack of self-control or underlying insecurities without taking responsibility.

According to our DNA, conflicting vibes turn people off unless they possess the same vibe with a magnetic gravitational pull. Otherwise, negative dialogue is kryptonic for the human psyche, even if we do not understand how it works or couldn't care less about its impact.

Thus, we must get our words right before mastering our physical or non-verbal touch or approach. What if we are already good with our words, touch, and approach? Congratulations. I am so proud of you! Thus, always keep in mind that trust is established or withdrawn the moment we open our mouths. So, it behooves us to remain gentle, loving, and kind.

When living by example, *As It Pleases God*, our approach is a powerful witness to those who do not yet know Christ. At the same time, it also serves as a beacon of hope and light to embrace the transformative power of God's Divine Love, the Bond of Perfection. Here is the Spiritual Seal from Colossians 3:14-15: *"But above all these things put on love, which is the bond of perfection. And let the peace of God rule in your hearts, to which also you were called in one body; and be thankful."*

In our Approach to Progress, what is up with the *As It Pleases God* stuff? By the Divine Grace of God, this MOVEMENT is about placing Him at the forefront and being about our Father's Business. Here is the Spiritual Seal: *"Let the word of Christ dwell in you richly in all wisdom, teaching and admonishing one another in psalms and hymns and spiritual songs, singing with grace in your hearts to the Lord. And whatever you do in word or deed, do all in the name of the Lord Jesus, giving thanks to God the Father through Him."* Colossians 3:16-17.

Thoughts of Progress

Do you believe that how you think matters in your progress? Do you feel that your thoughts are of your own? Do you question why you think the way you do? Do you take note of where those thoughts occur or come from? Do you know that your thoughts have invisible wings? Have you considered the fact that your thoughts are triggers? Once we align our thoughts with the Heavenly of Heavens, *As It Pleases God*, Revelation 12:14 becomes our example: *"But the woman was given two wings of a great eagle, that she might fly into the wilderness to her place, where she is nourished for a time and times and half a time, from the presence of the serpent."*

In the same way that our words are triggers, they can also become our protector once we align ourselves, *As It Pleases God*, and according to our Predestined Blueprint. Thus, with our Thoughts of Progress, we must get an understanding of them from a Divine Perspective to ensure that our mouths do not write transactional checks that our souls cannot cash. What does this mean? In all simplicity, what are your thoughts costing you? If you do not know, then it is time to get in the know.

Our thoughts are the hidden triggers behind the words we speak, shaping our actions, reactions, emotions, weaknesses, strengths, perceptions, perspectives, biases, and reality. Also, our thoughts release the same chemical compounds into the body as our words or touch would, with the same positive and negative effects. Really? Yes, really.

When dealing with our thoughts, this profound yet invisible trigger cannot be underestimated. How do we underestimate our triggers, especially when we are fully aware of who we are? Our thoughts are a GIFT of dualism that keeps on giving positively or negatively, allowing us the free will option to change, adjust, adapt, gravitate, or remain the same. For this reason, regardless of our level of awareness, these triggers are a part of our consciousness, which means we all have them.

More importantly, internal triggers give us the option to learn the differences associated with what we do, say, become, or the lack thereof, to determine our MINDSETS. Be it a positive mindset, a negative mindset, a Creative Mindset, a foolish mindset, or a blank mindset. We CHOOSE. *"For as he thinks in his heart, so is he."* Proverbs 23:7. Do we really have a choice in our thinking process? Absolutely.

Nothing would make it into reality unless it were a thought, meditation, or contemplation first. Spiritually, this is one of the reasons why Philippians 4:8 says, *"Finally, brethren, whatever things are true, whatever things are noble, whatever things are just, whatever things are pure, whatever things are lovely, whatever things are of good report, if there is any virtue and if there is anything praiseworthy—meditate on these things."*

When cultivating gentleness in our thoughts, we must become mindful of our judgments, mental chatter, false expectations, biases, and assumptions about ourselves and others. Although our thoughts are hidden, they do affect us Mentally, Physically, Emotionally, and Spiritually. Frankly, this is why Romans 12:2 tells us: *"And do not be conformed to this world, but be transformed by the renewing of your mind, that you may prove what is that good and acceptable and perfect will of God."*

The untamable aspects of the human mind are a force to be reckoned with, making self-correcting them mandatory in or out of the Kingdom of God. Why? Dualism resides in our minds, even if we do not want it there. What does this mean? The constant battle between right and wrong, just and unjust, good and bad, winning and losing, positive and negative, and so on, is always there, doing what they are designed to do.

The hidden thoughts we think can be harsh or judgmental unless we change the mental course of our thought process. If we fail to self-correct our thoughts from unrighteousness to righteousness, we will become abrasive, condescending, unkind, cruel, hateful, or rude by default.

Most of us think that we can beat the system or the duality of our thoughts without God; however, it creates disobedience, rebellion, idolatry, stiff necks, dullness, and lukewarmness instead. Majestically, this is why 2 Corinthians 10:4-5 says, *"For the weapons of our warfare are not carnal but mighty in God for pulling down strongholds, casting down arguments and every high thing that exalts itself against the knowledge of God, bringing every thought into captivity to the obedience of Christ."*

Unspokenly, we walk around thinking the Heaven on Earth Experience is a fairy tale, but as we can see, the duality of our thoughts is kicking us right in the gut! How so? First, it causes us to turn on ourselves without knowing it. Secondly, it makes us more sensitive, weak, emotional, combative, aggressive, and mushy than ever in the history of mankind. Thirdly, it causes us to forget about God, only to please ourselves while knowing nothing about the Fruits of the Spirit or behaving Christlike.

Our thoughts towards ourselves and others serve as the foundational catalyst for the behaviors, character traits, and attitudes we exude. How do we make this make sense, especially when attempting to do the right things in the Eye of God? First and foremost, attempting to do right does not necessarily make it right in the Eye of God. Secondly, if our negative chatter is out of control and we are lying to ourselves, it becomes difficult to hear ourselves think rationally. Thirdly, if our minds are clouded with known or unknown negativity, as a result, our words, touch, and approach will likewise be affected.

Even as Believers, once our thoughts are negatively clouded without correction or they lack purity, it creates tension from the inside out, hindering our open communication with ourselves or others. Then again, it may also affect our *Spirit to Spirit* Communion with our Heavenly Father until repentance, pruning, or purging occurs. Here is what James 3:17 tells us: *"But the wisdom that is from above is first pure, then peaceable, gentle, willing to yield, full of mercy and good fruits, without partiality and without hypocrisy."*

Meanwhile, in our dualism, built-in faculties, as it is with the negative, so it is with the positive. In the Eye of God, we must learn to reverse the negative to positive quickly without allowing it to simmer, manifest, or wreak havoc in our lives. By cultivating a mindset of gentleness, compassion, and understanding, we can nurture ourselves and others with a more positive and fulfilling bond of unity. So, *"Set your mind on things above, not on things on the earth."* Colossians 3:2.

Respect for Progress

God is respectful, and respectfulness is Godly. Respect the System of God, and it will respect us. Does this really matter? Absolutely. *"For by Him all things were created that are in heaven and that are on earth, visible and invisible, whether thrones or dominions or principalities or powers. All things were created through Him and for Him."* Colossians 1:16.

We become victims when we are disrespectful or violate natural and Spiritual Laws and Cycles. To remain in Divine Alignment, *As It Pleases God*, we should meditate *Spirit to Spirit*, worship Him in Spirit and Truth, and praise Him without screaming, yelling, fussing, or fighting. Why? They can sometimes carry unfavorable currency that we may not understand, depending upon our Spiritual Level or Status in the Eye of God.

Plus, embracing the Divine Presence is another reason that meditation is mentioned in the Bible multiple times. Is this Biblical? I would have it no other way. *"This Book of the Law shall not depart from your mouth, but you shall meditate in it day and night, that you may observe to do according to all that is written in it. For then you will make your way prosperous, and then you will have good success. Have I not commanded you? Be strong and of good courage; do not be afraid, nor be dismayed, for the LORD your God is with you wherever you go."* Joshua 1:8-9.

As ordained Shepherds designed to lead God's sheep, when operating with the Holy Spirit, we must establish ORDER, period. If we do not establish it, wolves in sheep's clothing will put a stench on our Divine Authority to Spiritually Govern, *As It Pleases God.*

Furthermore, we will never see an appointed judge not bringing order into the court first. After that, the moment disorder takes place, a penalty is levied. So, why is it that when operating with the Holy Spirit, we do not establish Divine Order, or if we do, we are put on blast? So, being that we are here...let us deal with this matter and how it affects our Creative Mindsets.

First, *"To everything there is a season, and a time for every purpose under heaven."* Ecclesiastes 3:1. Secondly, *"Walk in wisdom toward those who are outside, redeeming the time."* Colossians 4:5. And thirdly, *"Whoever has no rule over his own spirit is like a city broken down, without walls."* Proverbs 25:28.

How do we recognize when we are operating with broken-down walls in the Eye of God? There are many ways, but when we are master provokers, fire-starters, agitators, or instigators, we have work to do. How do we know if we are one of the above? Listed below are a few instances, but not limited to such:

- ☐ Feeling a sudden surge of anger, resentment, or frustration.
- ☐ An increase in heart rate and blood pressure.
- ☐ Feeling the need to defend yourself or your beliefs.
- ☐ Becoming defensive, hateful, or argumentative.
- ☐ Feeling a sense of tension or unease.
- ☐ Thoughts of revenge or retaliation.
- ☐ Feeling like you are being attacked or criticized.
- ☐ Hearing negative comments or insults.
- ☐ Feeling like you are being judged or evaluated unfairly.
- ☐ A desire to withdraw or avoid the situation.
- ☐ Feeling like you are being manipulated or controlled.
- ☐ Feeling like your boundaries are being violated.
- ☐ Experiencing a sense of helplessness.
- ☐ Thoughts of victimization or powerlessness.
- ☐ Feeling like you are not being heard or understood.
- ☐ A sense of injustice or unfairness.
- ☐ Feeling like your values or beliefs are being challenged.
- ☐ A sense of betrayal or mistrust.
- ☐ Feeling like you are being ganged up on or bullied.
- ☐ Feeling like you are being taken advantage of.
- ☐ A desire to stand up for yourself or fight back, even when wrong.

The goal is to become a problem-resolver, fire-douser, and solution provider. Although it may take a little bit of work, it is doable, primarily if you use the checklists available and applicable scriptures.

Our Creative Mindset is ready to be maximized, *As It Pleases God*. However, in the Realm of the Spirit, we must recognize our Spiritual Gifts, pursue our Spiritual Passions, learn and grow while Spiritually Tilling our own ground, take calculated risks, *As It Pleases God*, and pray for Divine Wisdom, Guidance, and Know-How. And, *"Whatever you want men to do to you, do also to them, for this is the Law and the Prophets."* Matthew 7:12.

The first step in building a Creative Mindset is to recognize the TALENTS and ABILITIES that God has given you, not the ones you trained yourself for or to become. We are all unique, and we all have something to offer the world with a Divine Blueprint attached to it. More importantly, no one is exempt from having a Predestined Blueprint hidden within them, even if they feel as if they have missed the mark. How do I know? Most often, our Spiritual Blueprint will hide within the battle scars and weaknesses that we hide, oppress, deflect, or suppress.

Take some time to reflect on your strengths and weaknesses, and think about how you can use them to glorify God and serve others. When recognizing the Creative Force that lies within, make sure that you: *"Repay no one evil for evil. Have regard for good things in the sight of all men. If it is possible, as much as depends on you, live peaceably with all men."* Romans 12:17-18.

Once you have identified your talents and abilities, it is essential to pursue your passions. Doing something that you love can bring a sense of purpose and fulfillment to your life. Whether it is painting, writing, singing, or cooking, find something that brings you joy, peace, contentment, and happiness, and commit to doing it regularly while incorporating God into the equation. Amid the pursuant process, *"Let no corrupt word proceed out of your mouth, but what is good for necessary edification, that it may impart grace to the hearers."* Ephesians 4:29.

Trusting The Process

To build a Creative Mindset and Trust The Process, you must be willing to learn and grow continually. You can take courses, attend workshops, read books, and seek out mentors who can help you develop your skills and expand your knowledge. All in all, patience, persistence, focus, and dedication are a few of the Spiritual Tools needed to move forward with Divine Creativity in the Spirit of Excellence.

What if we are tired, exhausted, and lack time? Then again, what about this scripture: *"Come to Me, all you who labor and are heavy laden, and I will give you rest."* Matthew 11:28. Spiritual Rest does not stop the MIND from working, nor does it prevent our fingers from documenting; more importantly, it does not nullify our Predestined Blueprint or Divine Creativity.

The bottom line is that we must seek rest IN HIM. Please allow me to Spiritually Align: *"Therefore, my beloved brethren, be steadfast, immovable, always abounding in the work of the Lord, knowing that your labor is not in vain in the Lord."* 1 Corinthians 15:58. In our works for the Lord, As It Pleases Him, we must know that our efforts are not in vain. Even when we face challenges or difficulties, we can trust in God's Divine Plan and Purpose without allowing our plans to get in the way.

Remember, perfection is not the goal. *"For all have sinned and fall short of the glory of God, being justified freely by His grace through the redemption that is in Christ Jesus."* Romans 3:23-24. Completion and diligence toward your Predestined Blueprint with what you have in your hands, *As It Pleases God*, is what is required of you, getting to the: *"Well done, good and faithful servant; you were faithful over a few things, I will make you ruler over many things. Enter into the joy of your lord."* Matthew 25:21.

In Trusting The Process, if you have it, use it for the Greater Good. *"And let the beauty of the Lord our God be upon us, And establish the work of our hands for us; Yes, establish the work of our hands."* Psalm 90:17.

When dealing with a Creative Mindset, if you do not have it, you DO NOT need it to do what you have been called to do...find another way! Why should a Believer find another way? When dealing with God, He is not limited. If He has to create a way out of no way, then consider it done and follow instructions, *As It Pleases Him*. Amid all, know this: "*And let us not grow weary while doing good, for in due season we shall reap if we do not lose heart.*" Galatians 6:9. Plus, He does not mind you using this scripture to hold Him ACCOUNTABLE. "*God is not a man, that He should lie, nor a son of man, that He should repent. Has He said, and will He not do? Or has He spoken, and will He not make it good?*" Numbers 23:19.

How can we hold God accountable? In the same way that you are held accountable for every word that proceeds out of the gateway of your mouth and your actions, being that you are created in His Divine Image, so is He. As the Heavenly of Heavens concurs, He is indeed accountable for His Divine Word. "*So shall My word be that goes forth from My mouth; it shall not return to Me void, but it shall accomplish what I please, and it shall prosper in the thing for which I sent it.*" Isaiah 55:11. Thus, you must place a DEMAND on it!

How can a Believer demand God? We do not demand Him, boss Him around, or prostitute Him as most attempt to do. We merely place a Spiritual Demand on the Word of God, use the Fruits of the Spirit as Divine Leverage, behave Christlike, cover ourselves with the Blood of Jesus as Spiritual Atonement, and remain in a Spiritual Classroom led by the Holy Spirit, becoming trained to feed His sheep, *As It Pleases Him*. What if this is a lot to do? It may appear as if there is a lot to do, but there is not!

Here is the deal: To simplify our efforts without trying to simplify God, we should begin with wholeheartedly praying, repenting, forgiving, and documenting in His Divine Presence while using the Fruits of the Spirit one by one for 30 days. For example:

- ☐ For the first three days, exhibit love.
- ☐ The next three days, exhibit love and joy.
- ☐ The next three days, exhibit love, joy, and peace.
- ☐ The next three days, exhibit love, joy, peace, and patience.
- ☐ The next three days, exhibit love, joy, peace, patience, and kindness.
- ☐ The next three days, exhibit love, joy, peace, patience, kindness, and goodness.
- ☐ The next three days, exhibit love, joy, peace, patience, kindness, goodness, and faithfulness.
- ☐ The next three days, exhibit love, joy, peace, patience, kindness, goodness, faithfulness, and gentleness.
- ☐ The remainder of the days exhibit love, joy, peace, patience, kindness, goodness, faithfulness, gentleness, and self-control.

Does this really work? Absolutely! I do not place a Divine Promise or Guarantee in an uncharted area or where I have not tread myself. Listen, the Fruits of the Spirit will transform the psyche from the inside out with humility and obedience that the Holy Spirit can work with, and the Blood of Jesus will suffice. What does this mean? We are all subjected to error; therefore, we must engage in a continual state of repentance to prevent the Holy Spirit from lying dormant and the misuse of the Blood of Jesus.

How can we misuse the Blood of Jesus? For example, when we loom curses over others in His Name for the same things that we are guilty of under a different label. Then again, we place our feet on someone's neck, proclaiming God said so. Due to the lack of Spiritual Discernment, we became His enemy because He was using the situation as a formal training ground for them. "*Therefore thus says the Lord God: 'Because you have spoken nonsense and envisioned lies, therefore I am indeed against you,' says the Lord God.*" Ezekiel 13:8.

As a result of becoming an enemy of God, we walk around looking like boo boo the fool with a Spiritual Woe for proclaiming what God DID NOT say. "*Woe to the foolish prophets, who follow their own spirit and have seen nothing!*" Ezekiel 13:3. Unfortunately, this is why we have recycled messages saying He said this or that, primarily when He is not speaking to them at all. "*And the Lord said to me: 'The prophets prophesy lies in My name. I have not sent them, commanded them, nor spoken to them; they prophesy to you a false vision, divination, a worthless thing, and the deceit of their heart.'* " Jeremiah 14:14.

When capitalizing on the Name of God with lies, deceit, and clickbait, it is only a matter of time before He pulls the rug from under the feet of our false prophets, self-chosen ones, and empty oracles. No pun intended; I am just the Messenger.

When dealing with Divine Creativity and Gifts of the Kingdom of God, we cannot play around with them, spread lies, or lack discernment. It can invoke the Wrath of God, and He will call us out in due time. Please allow me to Spiritually Align: "*The anger of the Lord will not turn back until He has executed and performed the thoughts of His heart. In the latter days you will understand it perfectly. I have not sent these prophets, yet they ran. I have not spoken to them, yet they prophesied.*" Jeremiah 23:21.

Do we not have free will to say and do whatever, whenever, and however? Absolutely! Nevertheless, exercising free will amid deceptive measures changes the rules of the ballgame and stunts our Spiritual Creativity. Unfortunately, this is why we have pilfering messages from others, proclaiming it is God. When in all actuality, He does not have to pilfer from anyone, period! He provides TRIGGERS to guide, inspire, motivate, direct, spark, and confirm, similar to putting gas in our cars.

If we are taking the whole car, then something is definitely wrong. The only difference here is pleasing ourselves and PLEASING GOD. Really? Yes, really! *"But if they had stood in My counsel, And had caused My people to hear My words, Then they would have turned them from their evil way And from the evil of their doings."* Jeremiah 23:22. If they had truly listened to His counsel and spoken His AUTHENTIC WORDS to the people, they would have led them away from sin and towards righteousness by default. Seeking God's Divine Wisdom and Guidance, *As It Pleases Him*, changes the trajectory of our lives from selfishness to selflessness with this Spiritual Approach.

If you desire to have a Creative Mindset, add God into the Equation, *As It Pleases Him*, with a WILLINGNESS to unveil your Predestined Blueprint. Is it that simple? Only God knows the level or intensity of the training needed for your Predestined Blueprint. But I will say this, 'It is much more challenging without Him—so choose your HARD wisely!'

Chapter 10

Take Risks

Creativity often requires taking risks and stepping out of your comfort zone. Playing it safe is not wise, and playing without God Almighty is more unwise. When placing Him at the forefront of our lives, *As It Pleases Him*, we do not need to be afraid to try new things, experiment with different techniques, or take on challenging projects.

Everything becomes a lesson, training, or testament toward polishing up your Creative Mindset and reason for being. Remember, failure is often a stepping stone to success, to create the ultimate win-win if you do not give up on God or yourself amid the journey.

Building a Creative Mindset that PLEASES God, bringing us in Purpose on purpose, is a lifelong journey. Still, it requires self-reflection, passion, learning, risk-taking, prayer, repenting, forgiveness, and tenacity. However, with God's help, we can all cultivate a Creative Mindset that allows us to live out our Divine Purpose and make a positive impact on the world around us. Moreover, empathy and understanding can help us recognize and connect with other perspectives and emotions, while cooperation and teamwork can help us collaborate and build upon each other's ideas. On the other hand, resourcefulness, people skills, and problem-solving skills can also help to overcome obstacles and find creative solutions to challenges or fine-tune what is already.

Developing a Creative Mindset can unlock endless possibilities in your life. Imagine having the ability to think outside of the box, take risks and embrace failure, collaborate with others, and share your ideas. All of this is possible when you cultivate a Creative Mindset, *As It Pleases God*. Here is your Creativity Checklist made simple:

- ☐ Take time to reflect on your experiences and thoughts.
- ☐ Seek feedback from God, *Spirit to Spirit*.
- ☐ Ask the Holy Spirit for help and guidance.
- ☐ Cover yourself and your thoughts with the Blood of Jesus.
- ☐ Document your ideas, thoughts, or feelings.
- ☐ Get around people who evoke your creativity.
- ☐ Enjoy hobbies or activities that spark your creativity.
- ☐ Read books, watch movies, and explore new ideas.
- ☐ Challenge yourself to think.
- ☐ Try new things and take risks.
- ☐ Practice repenting, forgiving, and meditation.
- ☐ Take breaks or a timeout.
- ☐ Allow yourself to daydream without distractions.
- ☐ Keep a journal or sketchbook close to you.
- ☐ Collaborate with others and share your ideas.
- ☐ Seek out feedback and critique to improve your work.
- ☐ Set goals and work towards them consistently.
- ☐ Embrace failure and use it as a learning opportunity.
- ☐ Stay curious and ask questions.
- ☐ Experiment with different ways of doing things.
- ☐ Take time to immerse yourself in nature.
- ☐ Keep an open, decluttered, and receptive mind.
- ☐ Focus on the process rather than the outcome.
- ☐ Practice self-care.
- ☐ Maintain a healthy work-life balance.
- ☐ Stay true to yourself and your unique creative vision.
- ☐ Use the Fruits of the Spirit.

☐ Behave Christlike at all times.

Why do we need a checklist as Believers? We do not need it; it is a guide to staying on track with our Spiritual Endeavors because our minds can quickly jump the track, going all the way to the left. Thus, the Creativity Checklist helps us reel the mind in and tame the psyche, *As It Pleases God*.

In the Eye of God, creativity is an essential component of our Heaven on Earth Experience. Still, being creative is not always easy or comfortable. Unfortunately, this is why many people struggle to come up with new ideas, think strategically, or establish original concepts and content. With this being said, keep in mind that we are all creative in some area, and it is our responsibility to pinpoint it and Spiritually Till that ground or area.

The first step in becoming the creative factor in your creative process is to understand that creativity is not something that happens by chance. We must avail ourselves of its release by learning, developing, and applying the skills associated with our Divine Alignment. This process requires training, testing, experimenting, and cultivating a willingness not to give up. While simultaneously challenging ourselves to pinpoint the win-wins that are in alignment with the Will of God, even amid seeming failure. Doing so develops a positive winning mindset, *As It Pleases Him*.

On the other hand, if we develop wins without Him, our Divine Creativity will become limited. Thus, we may need to glean from another man's Spiritual Reservoir due to the lack of courage and know-how to glean from our own Spiritual Negev (Underground Cistern).

Another critical factor in becoming Divinely Creative, *As It Pleases God*, is to add Him into our equational efforts, allow the Holy Spirit to guide us, and cover ourselves with the Blood of Jesus as Spiritual Atonement for our known and unknown frailties. Doing so allows us to develop a work-in-progress mentality, enabling our creative process to become Divine Inspiration.

How do we make this make sense? Simply put, God has a Divine Interest in us, and we are on a Divine Assignment. If not, we would not be here, nor would our Divine Assignment exist. Unfortunately, due to the Cycles and Vicissitudes of Life, we have forgotten the AGREEMENT.

The agreement? Yes, the Spiritual Agreement for the Heaven on Earth Experience. But do not worry; Spiritual Forgetfulness or the Divine Veil happens to everyone! Then again, all we need to do is AWAKEN from our slumber, *As It Pleases God*, and remain open-minded and receptive to the leading of the Spirit in total ONENESS.

Divine Wisdom, Understanding, and Guidance

As we journey through life, seeking Divine Wisdom, Understanding, and Guidance from the Heavenly of Heavens is an invaluable commodity that goes overlooked time and time again. Then again, developing a Creative Mindset, *As It Pleases God*, could become more tedious than we care to imagine, especially when coming under the subjection of the Holy Spirit.

Unbeknown to most, building a Creative Mindset takes intentional effort, resilience, and commitment. We must regularly seek inspiration and direction from God, *Spirit to Spirit*, to ensure that we are on the right path while documenting accordingly.

How do we connect *Spirit to Spirit* with our Heavenly Father? We begin with a designated meeting place for prayer, reading the Bible, meditating, repenting, forgiving, reviewing the use of the Fruits of the Spirit, and seeking Christlike Character updates. All of which require us to hold our tongues and seek counsel or correction from time to time.

What if we do not need correction? Unfortunately, we all stand to be corrected, and we all need to acknowledge that we cannot engage our Predestined Blueprint on our own. Plus, no one, and I mean no one, is 100% right or 100% wrong about every single thing. Why? There is human error within all of us, even if we pretend to be perfect. For this reason, we need repentance, forgiveness, mercy, prayer, gratefulness, the Fruits of the Spirit, the Blood of Jesus, and the Holy Spirit.

Regardless of how self-sufficient we think we are, we need God's help to develop a Creative Mindset that is PLEASING to Him. So, amid doing so, it is wise to pray for Divine Wisdom, Understanding, and Guidance as you seek to build a Creative Mindset. How do we go about doing so? You can begin by asking Him to reveal His plans for your life, how to use your talents and abilities for His glory, and how to take them from normal or average to Divine Status.

When we surrender our own desires, agendas, and plans to align with the Plan of God Spiritually, we will understand that His plan for us is far greater than anything we could imagine.

The Divine Print

The Divine Print is nothing more than God's Divine Stamp of Approval on us. To be clear, we are not required to have it, but the hidden desires within the psyche will long for it because we are created with it from the moment of conception.

We all have a longing for validation and purpose, and we cannot get to Divine Validation or Purpose without God Almighty. Is there a difference? Absolutely! We can validate ourselves and create a purpose for our own lives, but the longing for the Divine will remain within the psyche that keeps us secretly looking for something else. Meanwhile, once we step into the Divine, *As It Pleases God*, it has The Divine Print attached.

Once we come into this state of being, developing a *Spirit to Spirit* Bond, we must create a conducive environment for our Divine Creativity to flow. We must also have an undamned willingness to receive and an undistracted focus to connect to it. Does this work? Absolutely. I am living proof! For this reason, I am laying out The Divine Print to follow or connect to one's Predestined Blueprint, making life easier for those who are NEXT!

Once the guide is set, *As It Pleases God*, it is easier to follow the flow, pattern, or path of our Mindprint, Soulprint, Spiritprint, Creativeprint, and Blueprint. In making room for them, we must minimize distractions and create a space that is conducive to Divine Alignment and Creativity. Respecting The Divine Print, *As It Pleases Him*, will cause them to YIELD, especially when we put pen to paper (document). Whether it is a quiet room, a comfortable chair, an empty closet, or a specific type of music, find what works best for you and use it to create a space where you can focus and let Divine Creativity flow on your behalf.

Is it not a little selfish to seek solitude? All of your Spiritual Creativity already resides within you, and it is your responsibility to release it. Unfortunately, this task is not given to anyone else besides the one in which it dwells. Is this Biblical? I would have it no other way. *"And the Spirit and the bride say, 'Come!' And let him who hears say, 'Come!' And let him who thirsts come. Whoever desires, let him take the water of life freely."* Revelation 22:17. Your Spiritual Negev is already! If you do not know and understand this, your Divine Well will run dry due to the lack of knowledge. Nevertheless, it may take all of your experiences, traumas, mishaps, and disappointments to get you to the Spiritual Negev. But know this: IT IS THERE, awaiting your arrival!

So, if you give this responsibility away to another, it is your loss and their gain. How so? Ideas, thoughts, and beliefs are pilfered from those who do not realize the VALUE they possess from within or their inability to be patient, wait, prepare, and collaborate, *As It Pleases God*. Then again, it could be those who opt out of the Spiritual Classroom, refuse to use the Fruits of the Spirit and behave Christlike, or those who are trapped in a cycle of déjà vu because they refuse to forgive. But, of course, this is NOT you because you are reading this book right now, getting your wheels turning in the correct direction!

Power of Repentant Forgiveness

Forgiveness is the pathway to liberating redemption and Spiritual Renewal, *As It Pleases God*. Plus, it is also one of our hidden powers that will place a Spiritual Seal on our ability to move forward in the Spirit of Excellence before our Heavenly Father, even if people throw us away or kick us to the curb. *"If we confess our sins, He is faithful and just to forgive us our sins and to cleanse us from all unrighteousness."* 1 John 1:9.

The Power of Forgiveness is a GIFT to all mankind to help us break free from burdens and our past mistakes to establish reconciliation and transformation, *As It Pleases God*. In this process, we must also keep in mind that forgiveness is not the same as repentance. Using them together, *As It Pleases Him*, they have MORE bonding power when they are used together. Now, before we dive into the Power of Forgiveness, let us get an understanding of repentance first.

According to the Ancient of Days, repentance, alone at its core, is profound all by itself, even if we do not use it, abuse it, misunderstand it, or take it for granted. More importantly, it has enough transformative power that allow us to acknowledge our mistakes, take responsibility for our actions, and seek forgiveness, *As It Pleases God*. For this reason, it is imperative to understand how repentance works at a glance to preserve our Creative Mindsets in this lifetime and the next, but not limited to such:

- ☐ Repentance is shamelessly turning away from something or someone, *As It Pleases God*, through the process of confession.

- ☐ Repentance is having remorse for making a conscious choice to change, *As It Pleases God*, while admitting to mistakes, wrongdoings, or disappointments caused by us.

- ☐ Repentance is the reflective transformation of the negative impact caused by our behaviors, thoughts, beliefs, biases, words, and traumas, *As It Pleases God*.

- ☐ Repentance is confessing something to make the necessary changes needed to do the right thing in the Eye of God.

- ☐ Repentance is recognizing the shame, guilt, and fear associated with our hatefulness, unforgiveness, spitefulness, and competitiveness to make the changes necessary to rectify the harm caused.

- ☐ Repentance is allowing Divine Mercy to avail itself in our lives with humility and a willingness to confront our shortcomings, *As It Pleases God*.

- ☐ Repentance is paving the way for healing, restitution, and reconciliation by making amends for the harm caused, *As It Pleases God*.

- ☐ Repentance is making efforts to repair damaged relationships to restore balance and integrity, *As It Pleases God*.

- ☐ Repentance is making a sincere effort to address the root causes of whatever and with whomever to make a genuine change for the Greater Good, *As It Pleases God*.

- ☐ Repentance is making the meaningful adjustments needed to adjust our attitude and character, *As It Pleases God*.

- ☐ Repentance involves seeking forgiveness from those who have been wronged or lacked understanding of whatever, whenever, wherever, or however, *As It Pleases God*.

- ☐ Repentance assists in the restoration of trust and the rebuilding of relationships, creating opportunities for renewal, understanding, and mutual respect, *As It Pleases God*.

Repentance and forgiveness are vital components of our *Spirit to Spirit* Relations designed to safeguard our Creative Mindsets. In addition, it is also a fundamental aspect of our personal growth, professional astuteness, and moral development, regardless of whether we are good girls, bad girls, good boys, or bad boys.

The Power of God deals with our heart and mind postures and not the opinions or feelings of man. Why does He not consider our opinions or feelings? First, they cannot be trusted without Him. Secondly, when in a Spiritual Battle, the enemy will sow discord among the brethren, causing the root of bitterness, negative triggers, and underlying anger to keep us from possessing what rightly belongs to us. Then again, the enemy may also try to prevent us from helping or praying for those in need of help. Really? Yes, really! Remember, *"If a kingdom is divided against itself, that kingdom cannot stand. And if a house is divided against itself, that house cannot stand."* Mark 3:24-25.

If we desire to *Take Risks* for ourselves, we must forgive ourselves and others for whatever, whenever, and however. To be clear, no one, and I mean no one, is exempt from the Power of Forgiveness. Why is forgiveness non-exempting? There is enough mercy and hope for us all, especially when trying to do RIGHT in or out of the Kingdom. What if they continue to do wrong? Forgive them and give it to God. Their wrongness, debauchery, or ill will is not our burden to bear!

Most often, we overlook the basic things that God hates, condemning people for one thing while engaging in another. Thus, let us define them according to Proverbs 6:16-19. These six things the Lord hates, yes, seven, are an abomination to Him:

- ☐ A proud look.
- ☐ A lying tongue.
- ☐ Hands that shed innocent blood.
- ☐ A heart that devises wicked plans.
- ☐ Feet that are swift in running to evil.
- ☐ A false witness who speaks lies.
- ☐ And one who sows discord among brethren.

Each of these detrimental actions signifies moral and ethical deficiencies that are condemned and require repentance in the Eye of God. More importantly, before pointing the finger, it is only wise to use this checklist to make sure we are not operating in Spiritual Error under a different label.

Why must we do a checkup from the neck up as Believers? In all simplicity, due to the lack of understanding, here is how this works and why we need to repent and forgive consistently:

- ☐ Pride is one of the infamous snares also known as The Pride of Life, waiting to yoke us to the core, suppressing the humility required by the Kingdom of God.

- ☐ Deception and falsehood zap our authenticity, attempting to make us appear more than we are. Unfortunately, this makes us a magnet for lies, not being able to decipher the truth from untruths.

- ☐ The shedding or whitewashing of innocent blood represents violence, injustice, and disregard for the value of human life through our words, thoughts, actions, reactions, biases, beliefs, or manipulations. Be it Mental, Physical, Emotional, Spiritual, or Financial, in the Eye of God, they all have equal weight.

- ☐ Evil intentions and the scheming of the heart are hidden under jealousy, envy, pride, greed, coveting, competitiveness, plotting, selfishness, bullying, and contention. For the record, if we intentionally cause harm to ourselves or others, Mentally, Physically, Emotionally, Spiritually, or Financially, they all have equal weight in the Eye of God.

- ☐ Eagerly pursuing wickedness, idolatry, and being quick to engage in corrupt activities, displeasing to God, falls under swiftly running to evil. How so? When operating in willful disobedience, rebellion, lukewarmness, lying, chaos, dullness, unfruitfulness, stiffneckedness, debauchery, bullying, and ill-will, they all have equal weight in the Eye of God.

- ☐ Bearing false witness and spreading lies is a big no-no in the Eye of God. Belittling and putting down another to build ourselves up or using it as clickbait to destroy the lives of others is an abomination if it is not designed to speak justice, righteousness, and truth. In this matter, integrity and honesty are required of us to remain in the right standing with our Heavenly Father.

- ☐ If we are causing Mental, Physical, Emotional, Spiritual, or Financial conflict, division, or chaos among brethren, God views these behaviors as destructive, divisive, abusive, and debaucherous. Sowing discord in this manner is highly frowned upon by the Heavenly of Heavens.

All in all, before refusing to forgive, we must also remember to check our mindsets, perceptions, actions, reactions, and biases first. Why must we do this? The moment we find ourselves pointing the finger, we also must remember we have three fingers pointing back at us. With this understanding, know this: *"Judge not, and you shall not be judged. Condemn not, and you shall not be condemned. Forgive, and you will be forgiven."* Luke 6:37.

Thus, we must engage in checking ourselves first, resisting temptations, and choosing the path of righteousness. If we are engaging in the things that God hates, then we need to repent and forgive ourselves as well.

Why must we repent and forgive when doing things God hates? It develops our heart postures in one of two ways:

- ☐ A heart posture, *As It Pleases God*.

☐ A heart posture that DISPLEASES God.

What if we have committed the unforgivable? Whether we are the forgiver or the forgivee, forgiveness is our Spiritual Right from the Heavenly of Heavens. Once again, no one is exempt from asking for forgiveness or receiving it. Here is the Spiritual Decree: *"And whenever you stand praying, if you have anything against anyone, forgive him, that your Father in heaven may also forgive you your trespasses."* Mark 11:25.

What if we choose NOT to forgive? To answer this question, please allow me to take it to scripture: *"But if you do not forgive, neither will your Father in heaven forgive your trespasses."* Mark 11:26. Unfortunately, holding onto anger, hatefulness, grudges, and resentment is more burdensome than forgiving, letting go, letting God handle it, and moving on.

What if we forgive, and they do not change for the better? According to the Ancient of Days, it is NOT our responsibility to determine whether they change or not. We are responsible for our change with the use of the Fruits of the Spirit and Christlike Character Traits.

In the Realm of the Spirit, the Power of Forgiveness knows no limit, whereas unforgiveness sets limits. In light of this, it is our responsibility to choose our hard. For example: *"Then Peter came to Him and said, 'Lord, how often shall my brother sin against me, and I forgive him? Up to seven times?' Jesus said to him, 'I do not say to you, up to seven times, but up to seventy times seven.' "* Matthew 18:21-22.

If forgiveness does not occur, this negative emotion creates a magnetic effect, causing the same things we are not forgiving to find their way back to our house or Bloodline, hindering our personal growth and Spiritual Development. Then again, we can cause it to daunt, disappoint, or traumatize the psyche instead of freeing us to let go and let God.

Can we trust God in a matter when we forgive? Absolutely. Here is the Spiritual Contingency: *"Therefore 'If your enemy is hungry, feed him; If he is thirsty, give him a drink; For in so doing you will heap coals of fire on his head.' Do not be overcome by evil, but overcome evil with good."* Romans 12:20-21.

To avoid the recurrence of past mistakes, mishaps, traps, habits, or thirsts, we must let go of the fears, grudges, and resentments associated with being judged by others. We must also let go of the insecurities pertaining to being imperfect or flawed in the eyes of man. Above all, it helps us to release the anger and bitterness that have the potential to cloud or foggily taint our minds with people, places, and things having nothing to do with our Divine Blueprinted Purpose.

The opportunity for healing and reconciliation is within our reach, and all we need to do is grab hold of it to circumvent the toxic cycle or the vicious cycle of déjà vu from placing our lives in a tailspin. The moment we think this would not happen to us, rest assured that it is happening and in full effect! How is this possible when we are living our best lives? Our best lives are a matter of opinion, especially if we are Spiritually Blind, Deaf, and Mute to the things of God, to the Realm of the Spirit, or we our outright out of purpose.

Forgiveness does not mean that we condone or excuse our actions, words, beliefs, thoughts, or offenses that have provoked or caused pain on our behalf or that of another. In the Eye of God, it is all about making a conscious choice to repent and release the negative emotions associated with creating a win-win. More importantly, forgiveness is not for the sake of someone else; it is for our sake.

What if they do not accept our forgiveness? It is our responsibility to extend it sincerely, and if they do not accept, it is on them...We do not lose ground in the Eye of God. Know this: No man can create a Hell to put you in; only God can do that! I cannot tell you how many times I have been thrown away, kicked to the curb, and called everything but a Child of God, yet here we are!

Taking Risks to repent and forgive, *As It Pleases God*, cultivates greater self-awareness, integrity, and compassion that we can selflessly use to help someone else in our *Joint Ventures*. What does this mean? We cannot do what we do alone...thus, we need to use all of our Spiritual Tools to Grow Great in the Eye of God and man.

Before moving on to the next chapter, I want you to know that if no one forgives you, I forgive you...keep moving forward in the Spirit of Excellence. Pick yourself up, gird up your loins, learn from it, learn from them, learn from that, and keep moving forward, *As It Pleases God*. Yes, your past may indeed be DONE or OVER with. But no one knows what God is using to train you for your NEXT. In addition, you also may not know what or who He is using in or for your NOW! Besides, only you...Yes, you, can forfeit it! Really? Yes, really!

Your Spiritual Blueprint is already written, and you are the only one who can dismantle it or attempt to rewrite it. If you freely give someone else that much power over you to distract or disrupt your Divine Destiny, then it is on you! To keep this simple, you must ALIGN with your Destiny Helpers, not the Destiny Hinderers, Destroyers, or Fakers.

The greatest transformations indeed occur during the most challenging periods. Still, you should never intentionally add fuel to the fire. For sure, the power to give up on yourself lies within you, but so does the strength, courage, and tenacity to rise again with the Spirit of Determination cheering you on.

From me to you, despite all of the odds you have gone through, to say the least, you have seen and experienced too much to give up on yourself now. Remember, when living real life, setbacks, hiccups, and failures are inevitable. All of which are designed to test you, test them, or test that, to provide a repertoire of stepping stones or a TRAIL of Divine Wisdom to lead the way toward GREATNESS.

By viewing people, places, things, and events as Divine Preparation, *As It Pleases God*, you will become more apt to *Taking Risks* for Divine Enlightenment, Transformation, and Progress. With this open and guarded mindset, this outlook encourages you to see past the mundane and recognize the underlying purpose, wisdom, information, understanding, or whatever is hidden in the encounter or experience to glean for the Greater Good.

For this MOVEMENT of God, or better yet, in this *Joint Venture*, we leave no WILLING man behind. So, if you are still WILLING, keep reading; you have two more chapters to go, making your latter days greater than your former.

Chapter 11

Joint Ventures

Developing a Joint Venture in the Eye of God according to our Predestined Blueprint requires a deep understanding of our purpose, values, likes, dislikes, visions, traumas, weaknesses, and idiosyncrasies. Why is knowing about a joint venture essential to Believers? In connecting the connectable, they all come with triggers. Be it positive or negative, good or bad, right or wrong, just or unjust, and so on, a trigger is a trigger doing what it is designed to do with Spiritual Fruits or a debilitating dagger attached. Thus, we must know what they are or are not to avoid outing or turning on ourselves, especially when we do not get what we want, or we become disappointed due to false expectations appearing real.

How do we make a joint venture in the Eye of God make sense? To create a joint in anything or with anyone, we must know what it is or is not in order to connect or disconnect properly while getting a proper understanding, *As It Pleases God*. From the simplest things to the most complicated, if we are joining two things together as one, we must understand the growing, grafting, or merging process, including the Lower and Higher Laws associated.

For example, in Genesis 2:24, "*Therefore a man shall leave his father and his mother and hold fast to his wife, and they shall become one flesh.*" In a joint venturing process, if they do not become ONE, *As It Pleases God*, they will remain divided from the inside out until adding Him into the equation. Even if they pretend to be united behind closed doors, the truth will seep through the cracks like smoking vapors with a fruited stench.

How would we know the difference between whether we are united or divided? Once again, the difference is recognized in our FRUITS! Either they will become good, creating a cycle of growth, truth, valor, and goodness. Then again, if we leave God out of our equational or joint efforts, our fruits will become rotten, spoiling the whole bunch or traumatizing others with no remorse, creating a victim or woe-unto-me mentality and a trail of wounded victims, continuing the negative cycle.

Unfortunately, it is often the Spiritual Woes that cause us to turn on ourselves or unseal our Spiritual Seals. Do we not have the free will to unite or divide? Absolutely! We have the free will to do whatever, whenever, and however. According to the Heavenly of Heavens, we must also understand that negativity or debauchery does not come without consequences, regardless of our free-willed choices, status, fame, fortune, or whatever.

When engaging, it is only wise to lead with the Fruits of the Spirit at all times amid our joint or solo ventures. Here is what we must know: The Song of Solomon 8:6-7 says, "*Set me as a seal upon your heart, as a seal upon your arm, for love is strong as death, jealousy is fierce as the grave. Its flashes are flashes of fire, the very flame of the Lord. Many waters cannot quench love, neither can floods drown it. If a man offered for love all the wealth of his house, he would be utterly despised.*"

Harmonious Love

Harmonious Love is the Spiritual Glue or Seal that God requires of us. Why is this required, especially when we do not feel lovable? Feeling loved is a matter of perception, but GIVING LOVE is a PREREQUISITE for obtaining Spiritual

Treasures, Supernatural Protection, and Divine Wisdom of the Kingdom.

Why is Harmonious Love a prerequisite for Believers? Hatefulness is the one thing that melts us from the inside out, causing Spiritual Blockages of blindness, deafness, muteness, stiff necks, lukewarmness, and dullness. Meanwhile, if left ungoverned or uncorrected, it allows the psyche to take over as we appear right in our own eyes, creating an open door for compromise, yoking, and sifting. In addition, it also allows us to sugarcoat or downplay the Fruits of the Spirit as if it is NOT our Spiritual Lifeline to keep our joint communions lubricated, *As It Pleases God*. Please allow me to Spiritually Align: *"And above all these put on love, which binds everything together in perfect harmony."* Colossians 3:14.

Why is harmony so crucial in the Eye of God? Harmony has a rhythm of balance, cooperation, and unity between individuals, groups, and the environment. In the Eye of God, harmony fosters peace, love, and understanding of humanity, nature, and Spirituality. Whereas discord, conflict, confusion, lies, disagreements, opposing views, and division lead to suffering, judgment, biases, destruction, and turning on ourselves.

In the same way that we are connected to the Earth, we are connected to each other, even if we think we are not. Plus, with our multifaceted connections, we are also divided by Divine Limits and Spiritual Laws. For example, we are Spiritual Beings having a human experience in Earthen Vessels, regardless of whether we understand this process or not. Now, if we remove the Spirit, our vessel (the body) will go back to its owner, THE EARTH.

On the other hand, if we remove the vessel first, the Spirit must return to its owner, GOD. Are they not both the same? Unfortunately, they are not! Even though God is the Creator of it all, they both waver between a completed mission and an incomplete one of our choosing or free will, to be exact. *"For in Him all things were created: things in heaven and on earth, visible and invisible, whether thrones or powers or rulers or authorities; all things have been created through Him and for Him."* Colossians 1:16.

The mind is very fickle and can create anything it wants, positively or negatively. So, we must govern it accordingly to avoid dismantling other aspects of our being or causing any form of dysfunction. Can the mind really affect us? Yes, it can affect us positively or negatively. Then again, it can also infect us, causing our members to malfunction from the inside out. *"For as we have many members in one body, but all the members do not have the same function."* Romans 12:4.

According to the Heavenly of Heavens, when we ALIGN our goals and objectives with the Word of God, *As It Pleases Him*, we can truly achieve success and fulfillment to be about our Father's Business. What makes the Word of God so important to the life of a Believer? According to Hebrews 4:12, *"For the word of God is living and powerful, and sharper than any two-edged sword, piercing even to the division of soul and spirit, and of joints and marrow, and is a discerner of the thoughts and intents of the heart."*

The first step in developing a joint venture in the Eye of God is to seek His guidance, understanding, protection, and wisdom, *As It Pleases Him*, while using the Fruits of the Spirit and behaving Christlike. Why must we include Him? First, He has the Divine Blueprint. Secondly, it is through Him that we can avoid the cycle of déjà vu. Thirdly, to unveil our full potential, we must include Him in our equational efforts. If not, we will operate out of purpose or with half-portions, causing the psyche to pick up the slack or cover up for us.

In addition, we must pray for Spiritual Clarity, Unwavering Astuteness, and Divine Discernment, *Spirit to Spirit*, in our decision-making or training process. In whatever state or stage we are in, we must trust that He will lead us in the right direction without wavering.

In our Joint Ventures, it behooves us to seek the advice of Spiritual Mentors, Coaches, and Advisors who can provide us with insight, wisdom, understanding, and correction, *As It Pleases God*. Still, it is also essential to ensure that our Joint Venture is aligned with our Predestined Blueprint. If we do not know what it is, then it is time to get in the know, seeking Him, *Spirit to Spirit*, for Divine Alignment and Instructions.

Can we really seek God for this information? Absolutely! In our *Spirit to Spirit* alone time with our Heavenly Father, we only need to pray, repent, forgive, ask for understanding, remain calm, and document.

How do we know if we are documenting the correct information? Our alliances and documentation should be in line with our values, vision, and mission, leading us toward the Kingdom of God and not away from it. Thus, we must be clear about our goals, wants, needs, desires, and objectives to ensure that our endeavors are consistent with our purpose, passion, and calling. Why? To Spiritually Align it with the Word of God and to TEST the Spirit behind whatever, whomever, and however. God does not mind at all...Plus, He has enough know-how, how-to, and power to confirm and align, *As It Pleases Him*.

Plus, if it displeases Him, then we already know who is behind it, them, or that...so we need to look for the win-win or reverse it from negative to positive, bad to good, wrong to right, unjust to just, and so on.

What if we do not know how to reverse the effect? It is time to learn the opposite of words in our vocabulary. No pun intended...we need to know this for real! Why? Most of us do not really know what is positive or negative, right or wrong, just or unjust, and so on.

How could we not know, especially when we are well-spoken? Being well-spoken is not what God is expecting from us...He wants us to recognize, align, and reverse according to the Fruits of the Spirit.

With all due respect, if we are well-spoken and do not know how to use the Fruits of the Spirit in our people skills, we are doing a disservice to ourselves. Why? Our words should become smooth as butter and sweet as honey, positively penetrating the psyche of another. If we are leaving someone untouched, traumatized, or uninspired, we have work to do.

How do we work on ourselves, especially when everyone is different? Understandably, we are all different, but the Spirit of man and the psyche respond to the Fruits of the Spirit across the board. Here are the essential virtues of the Fruits of the Spirit that every Believer should strive to cultivate on a moment-by-moment basis according to Galatians 5:22-23:

- ☐ Love.
- ☐ Joy.
- ☐ Peace.
- ☐ Patience.
- ☐ Kindness.
- ☐ Goodness.
- ☐ Faithfulness.
- ☐ Gentleness.
- ☐ Self-Control.

Just keep in mind that by incorporating these qualities, this cheerful and kind approach can become intimidating to those who are secretly or openly insecure or hostile and who may not know any better. Still, it is our responsibility to lead in the Spirit of Love and Excellence.

Why should we be kind to malignant, nasty, and rude people? Because the Fruits of the Spirit are gleanable, relatable, memorable, and penetrable, perfecting our Christlike Character, *As It Pleases God*. Plus, we do not want to become like them or similar to a person in Proverbs 25:28:

"Whoever has no rule over his own spirit is like a city broken down, without walls."

Without pointing the finger or putting anyone on blast, the goal is to obey the GREATEST COMMANDMENTS: *"And you shall love the Lord your God with all your heart, with all your soul, with all your mind, and with all your strength.' This is the first commandment. And the second, like it, is this: 'You shall love your neighbor as yourself.' There is no other commandment greater than these."* Mark 12:30-31.

In doing so, it is also essential to establish clear communication and transparency in our Joint Ventures. We must be honest and upfront with our partners about our expectations, limitations, and challenges. We should also be open to feedback and suggestions from our partners, as this can help us to improve and grow as individuals and as a team.

How can the Fruits of the Spirit assist us in this matter? All in all, it helps us develop our people skills by knowing how to conduct ourselves from the inside out. Here are a few tips, but not limited to such:

- ☐ Love others unconditionally.
- ☐ Show kindness and compassion.
- ☐ Exhibit patience and understanding.
- ☐ Practice self-control in difficult situations.
- ☐ Demonstrate joy and gratitude.
- ☐ Strive for peace and harmony in relationships.
- ☐ Show generosity and give freely to others.
- ☐ Display gentleness and humility in interactions.
- ☐ Be faithful and trustworthy in commitments.
- ☐ Practice forgiveness and let go of grudges.
- ☐ Be honest and transparent in all communications.
- ☐ Encourage and uplift others with words.
- ☐ Serve others with a joyful heart.
- ☐ Be a good listener and empathize with others.
- ☐ Show respect and honor to all people.
- ☐ Practice contentment and gratefulness.

- ☐ Avoid envy, pride, jealousy, or greed.
- ☐ Choose to be hopeful and repent often.
- ☐ Be a peacemaker and resolve conflicts quickly.
- ☐ Live a life of purpose and meaning, guided by faith and love.

Spirit of Humility and Servant Leadership

Another crucial element of developing a Joint Venture in the Eye of God is to maintain a Spirit of Humility and Servant Leadership. We should be willing to serve others and put their needs and interests ahead of our own, *As It Pleases God*. We should also be willing to admit our mistakes, apologize, and seek forgiveness when necessary.

Why should we jump through hoops when someone is taking our kindness for a weakness? Unbeknown to most, kindness is not a weakness...it is a HIDDEN STRENGTH that can cause a Legion of Angels to swoop in to save us at the drop of a dime. How is this possible? It gives us Spiritual Leverage when used correctly or when someone has their foot on our necks, attempting to yoke us to the core.

When kindness is used *As It Pleases God*, we are not required to seek revenge, correct, or fix anyone...if we fix ourselves and set a guard over our tongues and minds, *As It Pleases Him*, He will take care of what belongs to Him and us. Simply put, a seed will take care of itself, positively or negatively. All we need to do is ensure that we are sowing good seeds and uprooting the bad instead of watering them. However, if we do not know this, we will find ourselves playing god in our lives and the lives of others due to selfishness. What is the big deal? It takes the same amount of energy to approach all things with a humble and selfless demeanor, with God Almighty at the forefront.

When the VIRTUES of the Holy Spirit lead us, we can use the Fruits of the Spirit as Divine Leverage and Spiritual

Covering, even if we are not perfect. How is this possible? No one is perfect, even if we pretend we are. We are all a work-in-progress, and if we humbly develop a *Spirit to Spirit* Relationship with our Heavenly Father, pray, forgive, repent, use the Fruits of the Spirit, behave Christlike to the best of our ability, cover ourselves with the Blood of Jesus as Spiritual Atonement, and allow the Holy Spirit to guide, Divine Transformation is inevitable. In addition, if we document, *As It Pleases God*, we can also gain Supernatural usable Power and Favor. As a matter of fact, we gain more leverage than those who do nothing at all, who are rebellious and disobedient, or who could give a rat's tail about Him, the Kingdom, or their Divine Blueprint.

The Bonding Factors

Once again, we must KNOW the above information in order to ENFORCE it or place a Spiritual Demand. In my opinion, this is similar to water having the potential to become ice, but it must be placed in the right conditions of a Higher Law (Put in the freezer at 32°F or lower) to enforce it.

How does a Higher Law govern this or apply to us? First, ice freezes from the top down, similar to the mind governing our bodily functions, because we, too, are composed mostly of water. On average, the human body is composed of about 60% water. However, this percentage can vary depending on factors such as age, sex, and body composition. Secondly, the laws of thermodynamics govern the process of freezing, which involves the transfer of energy from the water to its surroundings, providing a useful framework for understanding the behavior of energy and entropy in the process of freezing ice.

If we take this a little further, freezing is based on two key factors: the physical properties of water and the behavior of molecules. Water is a unique substance that has three states of matter: solid (ice), liquid (water), and gas (water vapor), similar to the Mind, Body, Soul, and Spirit anomaly.

How do we make this make sense? When water freezes, the molecules slow down and begin to form a lattice structure. This process starts at the surface of the water, where the temperature is cooler than the water below. As the temperature drops, the molecules begin to form bonds with each other, creating a solid layer of ice on the surface. The reason why ice forms on the surface first is due to the behavior of molecules. Water molecules are constantly moving and colliding with each other. When the temperature drops, the molecules move more slowly and are more likely to form bonds with each other.

In the same way, the behavior of molecules affects the formation, liquidity, or gas through the strengthening and weakening of molecular bonds when dealing with water; we are no different with our thoughts, words, actions, and desires affecting or determining our people skills.

According to the Heavenly of Heavens, it is the Fruits of the Spirit that help us remain balanced with an internal Spiritual Negev, preventing our minds and hearts from becoming stone-cold, crystalized, slushy mushy, or all over the place.

What are the indications of needing to fine-tune our people skills? Listed below are a few indicators, but not limited to such:

- ☐ Difficulty in communicating effectively with others.
- ☐ Inability to build and maintain positive relationships.
- ☐ Tendency to dominate conversations.
- ☐ Constantly interrupting others.
- ☐ Inability to listen actively and empathetically.
- ☐ Insensitivity to others' feelings and needs.
- ☐ Tendency to criticize, blame, or judge others.
- ☐ Difficulty in giving and receiving feedback.
- ☐ Inability to resolve conflicts effectively.

- ☐ Lack of awareness of one's own emotions.
- ☐ Disregard how one's behaviors affect others.
- ☐ Inability to manage stress and emotions healthily.
- ☐ Tendency to avoid difficult conversations.
- ☐ Avoid confronting relevant issues.
- ☐ Inability to adapt.
- ☐ Cannot communicate with different personalities.
- ☐ Difficulty in understanding others.
- ☐ Not respecting cultural differences.
- ☐ Inability to manage time and priorities effectively.
- ☐ Tendency to micromanage or control others.
- ☐ Lack of accountability and responsibility.
- ☐ Inability to delegate tasks and responsibilities.
- ☐ Tendency to avoid taking risks or trying new things.
- ☐ Inability to motivate and inspire others.
- ☐ Lack of self-awareness and personal growth.
- ☐ Having a history of leaving rotten fruits behind.
- ☐ Being rude or insulting others with zero remorse.
- ☐ Possessing the inability to share with others.
- ☐ Feeling entitled.
- ☐ Willfully violating the boundaries of others.

Suppose we allow these character traits to penetrate the Mind, Body, Soul, or Spirit. In this case, we will struggle with envy, jealousy, pride, greed, coveting, and competitiveness, subjecting ourselves to the Dualism of Envy and Jealousy without understanding how it evolved.

Dualism of Envy and Jealousy

Do you feel insecure about your accomplishments? Do you compare yourself to others? Do you feel as if you have to outdo someone else? Do you work overtime to become better than someone? Do you feel as if another person threatens your worth? Do you celebrate the accomplishments of others? Are you happy when people succeed?

As the clock keeps ticking from Genesis to Revelation, we as a people need to get a grip on the slivers of envy and the whispers of jealousy, combating their toxic effects. 1 Corinthians 3:3 says, *"For you are still carnal. For where there are envy, strife, and divisions among you, are you not carnal and behaving like mere men?"*

From the Garden of Eden, Adam and Eve had a *Spirit to Spirit* Connection of purity, innocence, and being Spiritually Veiled from dualism without having to struggle with opposing forces until doubt was introduced to them. As a result of their acts of disobedience, they went from being Spiritually Veiled, *As It Pleased God*, to being unveiled for DISPLEASING Him through their willful acts associated with jealousy, envy, pride, greed, and coveting.

As a result of these unchecked character traits exposed by disobedience, Adam and Eve had their nakedness, Mentally, Physically, Emotionally, and Spiritually uncovered to dualism, which included an ongoing struggle with opposing forces and shamefulness. And, now, with our Religious selves, we have the nerve to debate about who is right or who is wrong about whether they knew about good and evil prior to partaking in the Forbidden Fruit debacle. Not having a clue about the Spiritual Veil that existed, nor understanding how it works according to the Heavenly of Heavens, and the necessity to heed Divine Instructions. Above all, not knowing this: *"But if you bite and devour one another, beware lest you be consumed by one another!"* Galatians 5:15.

To be clear, once again, Adam and Eve were Spiritually Veiled with Divine Instructions on what to do and what not to do. And so are we! Plus, Adam and Eve are not doing any more than we are doing now. Just look around. Can you not see? See what? The disobedience! Due to the reason of known and unknown disobedience, we are Spiritually Veiled from the Divine Treasures, Secrets, Understanding, and Wisdom due to our rebellious nature until we exhibit obedience, *As It Pleases God.*

For the record, we can never put a human perspective on a Divine Perspective because we will get it wrong every single time. Here is what Isaiah 55:8-9 says, " *'For My thoughts are not your thoughts, nor are your ways My ways,' says the Lord. 'For as the heavens are higher than the earth, so are My ways higher than your ways, and My thoughts than your thoughts.'* "

Unfortunately, we remain Spiritually Veiled to this very day. Blasphemy, right? Wrong. When dealing with the nature of the beast, we do not know if we are Spiritually Veiled until we are UNVEILED. Picturesquely, this is similar to falling asleep...we do not know that we are asleep until we are awakened or catch ourselves dozing off.

Then again, in the same way, we are veiled from our Predestined Blueprint until we are Spiritually Trained to possess it, *As It Pleases God.* Dualism is veiled as well. What does this mean? Most people of today do not really know the opposite or the consequences of what they are doing, saying, or becoming due to the Spiritual Veil blocking them. Moreover, they do not realize that they must willfully break this blockage by reversing the dualism effect.

How do we make the dualism effect make sense? The same way the Spiritual Veil existed, protecting Adam and Eve from dualism before disobedience and doubt occurred in the Garden of Eden. The reverse is now happening as we are Spiritual Blind to the reality of it. Simply put, in the dualism effect, instead of the Spiritual Veil protecting us, it blocks us until we are WILLING and READY to use it the way God intended from the Beginning.

Here is the deal: Dualism is two opposing principles or forces and a contrast between good and evil, right and wrong, and so on. But, for this section, we are going to deal with the Dualism of Envy and Jealousy.

Whether we embrace or reject dualism, our Mind, Body, Soul, and Spirit depend on it because doubt tries to prevent us from understanding how to self-correct, *As It Pleases God*. Only to instigate self-projection to please ourselves or satiate an agenda. Unfortunately, we will 'get got' if we do not know the opposite of what we are doing, saying, or becoming.

We have been deceived by a sliver and a whisper from the enemy's camp. As we have it today, we are falling into the hidden trap of comparison, jealousy, and envy. If one does not believe it, then look around...it is not a secret. Since the rise of social media, we have been barraged with superficial images and delightful stories of success, happiness, and perfection to get our palates wet. But my question is, 'Where is God in all of this?'

Most of us think the Forbidden Fruit or the Tree of Good and Evil is played out, overrated, or does not exist. Nevertheless, Galatians 5:19-21 brings us up to speed on the relevant ways we throw ourselves out to the wolves or turn on ourselves without knowing it. *"Now the works of the flesh are evident, which are: adultery, fornication, uncleanness, lewdness, Idolatry, sorcery, hatred, contentions, jealousies, outbursts of wrath, selfish ambitions, dissensions, heresies, envy, murders, drunkenness, revelries, and the like; of which I tell you beforehand, just as I also told you in time past, that those who practice such things will not inherit the kingdom of God."*

All of these will cause the Spiritual Veil to remain unless we repent and use the Fruits of the Spirit, the assistance of the Holy Spirit, and the Blood of Jesus for Spiritual Atonement. Will this work in removing the Spiritual Veil? Absolutely, especially if we make our wholehearted best attempts toward becoming and remaining righteous. Here is the Spiritual Seal that we can leverage: *"I say then: Walk in the Spirit, and you shall not fulfill the lust of the flesh. For the flesh lusts against the Spirit, and the Spirit against the flesh; and these are contrary to one another, so that you do not do the things that you wish. But if you are led by the Spirit, you are not under the law."* Galatians 5:16-18.

So, you see, without God, it becomes very difficult to differentiate between authentic and fake. And being that we lack the dualism related to this matter, the enemy places seeds of doubt to evoke envy and jealousy from within the human psyche with a thought, question, or image. The slithers of envy and whispers of jealousy happened in Genesis 3:1-7, and it is still happening to this very day.

The feelings of inadequacy, envy, and jealousy are real human emotions that no one is exempt from having. The key is to know what to do when they present themselves. Suppose they are left unchecked, or we do not pinpoint the underlying reason. In this case, they can fester, turning into resentment, bitterness, ungratefulness, or hatefulness. Once this happens, unfortunately, it creates an unfair advantage in all things Spiritual.

Why do we have an unfair advantage as Believers, especially when it comes to envy and jealousy? From the first family of Adam and Eve, this plague follows us until we reverse or cancel it.

Envy and jealousy are emotions that are often used interchangeably; however, they are not the same. They actually have different meanings and implications that we are going to unveil.

Envy is when we want, desire, or demand to have something belonging to someone else. Be it tangible or intangible! If we lust after, plot for, or degrade others for possessions, a quality, status, person, place, thing, or an achievement, envy is involved. If this feeling is not dealt with through repentance, forgiveness, and thanksgiving, it can lead to resentment, inadequacy, inferiority, or bitterness about someone else's stuff.

Jealousy, on the other hand, stems from fear or threat. The fear or threat of losing, the fear or threat of missing out, the fear or threat of abandonment, the fear or threat of whatever. All of these may involve feelings of insecurity, possessiveness, protectiveness, watchfulness, or suspicion over something or someone BELONGING TO US. However, this usually occurs in relationships, but is not limited to such. We can allow jealousy to drive us wild, or we can allow it to drive us WISE.

To be clear, if something or someone DOES NOT belong to us or we cannot lay claim to it or them, it falls under envy. If something or someone belongs to us or we consider our own, it is jealousy!

Why do we need to know the difference? When dealing with the root of a matter, we need to know the difference to avoid becoming sucker-punched with idolatry. I will repeat that envy falls into the category of idolatry.

For example, if we have a desire, lust, intense focus, devotion, or simply fighting for a golden calf that is not ours...have we not made an idol out of it? Absolutely. Unhealthy obsessions in the Eye of God will cause us to turn on ourselves from the inside out. Why? *"Thou shall have no other gods before me."* Exodus 20:3. Need I say more? Yes, I should! *"You shall not bow down to them nor serve them. For I, the Lord your God, am a jealous God, visiting the iniquity of the fathers upon the children to the third and fourth generations of those who hate Me."* Exodus 20:5.

Before ending this chapter, let us get an understanding of an idol for a moment to prevent a generational curse from being imposed on the innocent. This deeply rooted concept of transference is similar to how we are suffering the consequences of Adam and Eve's decisions from back then to now.

Here is the deal: An idol is an obsession, fixation, or fascination with something or someone, taking on many forms, from a physical object to a person, place, thought, power, money, sex, fame, or even an idea. The bottom line is that idolatry is not confined to a person or object. It is whatever has a powerful influence over our lives, shaping our values, priorities, and aspirations, leading us away from the Kingdom or our Blueprinted Mission to become self-serving and self-seeking. Clearly, these things can drive us to achieve, and they can lead us astray as well. Therefore, we must put all things into their proper perspective, *As It Pleases God*.

On the other hand, when becoming too attached, envy and jealousy have a way of positioning us to take insults or become character assassinated. Why would this happen? It is designed to redefine us to their liking due to an underlying identity crisis. In idolistic nefariousness, if we DO NOT know ourselves from the inside out or *As It Pleases God*, we will fall for the okey-doke.

When people, including our idols, start to insult us...We must back up from the situation instead of engaging. Should we not stand up for ourselves? In the same way that the serpent got into Eve's head to plant seeds of doubt, debasement, and superiority, the same can happen to us if we engage. Galatians 6:3-5 says, *"If anyone teaches otherwise and does not consent to wholesome words, even the words of our Lord Jesus Christ, and to the doctrine which accords with godliness, he is proud, knowing nothing, but is obsessed with disputes and arguments over words, from which come envy, strife, reviling, evil suspicions, useless wranglings of men of corrupt minds and destitute of the truth, who suppose that godliness is a means of gain. From such withdraw yourself."*

We are to respect, *As It Pleases God*, and not idolize to please ourselves. Here are a few ways to protect ourselves when veering from idolatry, but not limited to such:

- ☐ Align all things with the Word of God.
- ☐ Add God into your equational efforts.
- ☐ Trust your instincts.
- ☐ Use the Fruits of the Spirit, and behave Christlike.
- ☐ Pray for Spiritual Discernment.
- ☐ Pay attention to red flags.

- ☐ Do not violate your conscience.
- ☐ Recognize when something feels off.
- ☐ Set clear boundaries and stick to them.
- ☐ Communicate effectively and openly.
- ☐ Convey your needs and feelings.
- ☐ Practice self-awareness and reflection.
- ☐ Understand your vulnerabilities.
- ☐ Seek support when needed.
- ☐ Educate yourself about manipulation tactics.
- ☐ Become astute at recognizing deception.
- ☐ Take time to consider decisions.
- ☐ Do not be pressured into anything.
- ☐ Govern your thoughts and actions.
- ☐ Avoid engaging in power struggles.
- ☐ Engage in healthy communication.
- ☐ Learn to say no.
- ☐ Do not fall for a guilt trip.
- ☐ Surround yourself with positive influences.
- ☐ Keep a journal to track patterns and behaviors.
- ☐ Develop a strong sense of self-worth and confidence.
- ☐ Take steps to distance yourself from negativity.
- ☐ Avoid manipulative tactics.
- ☐ Focus on personal growth and self-improvement.
- ☐ Reverse any negative self-talk to positive.
- ☐ Question your doubts and fears.
- ☐ Do not violate boundaries.

The goal is to be happy and content with our own stuff, and "*If we live in the Spirit, let us also walk in the Spirit. Let us not become conceited, provoking one another, envying one another.*" Galatians 5:25-26. Besides, if we have tapped into our Predestined Blueprinted Purpose or Creative Mindset, we would not have time to become envious of another. Instead, we would focus on perfecting our own Creative Playbook.

CHAPTER 12
Creative Playbook

The Creative Playbook from the Heavenly of Heavens is a powerful maneuvering technique to use in our approach to being about our Father's Business. It is also used in connecting the Spiritual Rivers of our past, present, and future. The continuity and interconnectedness of our Spiritual Experiences and Journeys throughout time make us who we are today, connecting us to our daily portions. Above all, according to the Ancient of Days, there is always a Creative Playbook left behind, full of Divine Wisdom and Instructions for our NEXT.

In the Book of Genesis, in the Garden of Eden, Four Rivers flowed through it: Pishon, Gihon, Tigris, and Euphrates. In our Creative Playbook, we have a connecting flow to our Predestined Blueprint and our Tree of Life, uncovering the secrets of ourselves, the Kingdom, and our Heaven on Earth Experiences. The Four Rivers represent the flow of life, the test of time, constant provisions, and expended energy for:

- ☐ Wisdom.
- ☐ Knowledge.
- ☐ Understanding.
- ☐ Experiences.

Life is designed to TEST us in these four areas to get our Spiritual Rivers to flow properly to facilitate and shape the Tree of Life from within each of us.

What if we omit the Spiritual Rivers of our Creative Playbook? We have free will to accept or reject anything we like. Nor do I force this upon anyone; I am just the Messenger. But, yes, there is a but in this matter...know this: *"Then the third angel sounded: And a great star fell from heaven, burning like a torch, and it fell on a third of the rivers and on the springs of water. The name of the star is Wormwood. A third of the waters became wormwood, and many men died from the water, because it was made bitter."* Revelation 8:10-11.

According to the Heavenly of Heavens, the Divine Wisdom passed down from our Forefathers should not be taken for granted. Nor should we send our minions out to destroy the LEGACIES of the Fraternal Blueprint set in stone that has been passed down through generations. As the Elements of the Unknown continue to shape our present and future, it is time to wake up and set our houses in order, *As It Pleases God.*

Why must we bring balance to the Four Rivers and our homes as Believers? The Spiritual Unrest is shaking us to the core because of the attempt to stop the Eternal Flow of what is Spiritually Guarded and Protected by the PRAYERS of our Forefathers. Blasphemy, right? Wrong. *"And the smoke of the incense, with the prayers of the saints, ascended before God from the angel's hand. Then the angel took the censer, filled it with fire from the altar, and threw it to the earth. And there were noises, thunderings, lightnings, and an earthquake. So the seven angels who had the seven trumpets prepared themselves to sound."* Revelation 8:4-6.

The moment we take a Spiritual Battle and make it a battle of wits and a play on words to deflect and project chaos, bitterness, hatefulness, and mass manipulation, it sounds the Spiritual Trumpets from the Heavenly of Heavens. Really? Yes, really!

Unbeknown to most, the Spiritual Trumpets can only be heard by the Spiritual Elites with the Spiritual Ears to hear from the Heavenly of Heavens. In addition, it places a Spiritual Seal on Revelation 2:7. *"He who has an ear, let him hear what the Spirit says to the churches. To him who overcomes I will give to eat from the tree of life, which is in the midst of the Paradise of God."*

Why them? Do we not all have the right to hear the Divine Trumpets as Believers? Absolutely. However, we must become Spiritually Trained, Tested, and Unveiled, *As It Pleases God*, in dualism and silence with Kingdom Protocols and Ethics. Please allow me to Spiritually Align: *"When He opened the seventh seal, there was silence in heaven for about half an hour. And I saw the seven angels who stand before God, and to them were given seven trumpets."* Revelation 8:1-2. *"And I looked, and I heard an angel flying through the midst of heaven, saying with a loud voice, 'Woe, woe, woe to the inhabitants of the earth, because of the remaining blasts of the trumpet of the three angels who are about to sound!'"* Revelation 8:13. If you think for a moment that this is not upon us right now, or it is a joke, then think again!

Now, using our Creative Playbook selfishly or oppressing others without the Holy Trinity will cause it to lose its creative effects and become an ordinary book of play. What type of book is this? It is when we play ourselves short. Then again, it may cause us to become a Tree of Death. Regardless of where we are right now, let us understand these Four Rivers of our Creative Playbook before going deeper.

The Pishon River is said to have flowed around the land of Havilah, where there was gold, bdellium (a fragrant resin), and onyx stones. Some scholars believe that the Pishon may have been located in modern-day Arabia, while others place it in Ethiopia. Regardless of the location of this precious river, the Spiritual Principle is beyond rationalizing and questioning. Here is the deal: River Pishon is associated with

ABUNDANCE and PROSPERITY and is seen as a symbol of God's Divine Blessings.

The Gihon River is said to have flowed through the land of Cush, which is believed to be modern-day Ethiopia. According to some interpretations, the Gihon may have actually been the Nile River, which was known for its life-giving waters. The Gihon is often associated with the idea of RENEWAL and REJUVENATION, which is why it is associated with Spiritual Growth and Enlightenment.

The Tigris River is one of the two great rivers of Mesopotamia, and it is still a major waterway in modern-day Iraq. The Tigris is associated with the concept of WISDOM and KNOWLEDGE, marking our Creative Playbook for intellectual growth, regrafting, and understanding. In the Bible, the Tigris is mentioned as the river that flowed out of the Garden of Eden and watered the land of Assyria.

The Euphrates River is another great river in Mesopotamia, and it is also a major waterway in modern-day Iraq. The Euphrates is associated with the idea of POWER and AUTHORITY, marking our Creative Playbook of charactorial influence and people skills. In the Bible, the Euphrates is mentioned as the river that flowed out of the Garden of Eden and watered the land of Babylon.

So, what is the connection between these Four Rivers and the Tree of Life? One interpretation is that each of these rivers represents a different aspect of life and existence, and that the Tree of Life is the SOURCE of all of these aspects. In this way, the Tree of Life is seen as a symbol of the UNITY and INTERCONNECTEDNESS of all things.

What if we avoid becoming interconnected, *As It Pleases God*? Once again, we have free will to do whatever, whenever, however, wherever, and with whomever. Still, Revelation 16:4-6 reminds us of this fact: *"Then the third angel poured out his bowl on the rivers and springs of water, and they became blood. And I heard the angel of the waters saying: "You are righteous, O Lord, The One who is and who was and who is to be, Because You have judged these things. For they have shed the blood of saints and prophets, And You have given them blood to drink. For it is their just due."* Whether we are dealing with our Four Rivers or the Tree of Life, if we use the Fruits of the Spirit and behave Christlike, *As It Pleases Him*, our 'just due' will always be of GOOD in the Eye of God. If we opt not to use them, then our 'just due' becomes questionable.

Let us recap a few items that we must make sure we capitalize on in our Creative Playbook, nourishing our Tree of Life, but not limited to such:

- ☐ Renewal.
- ☐ Rejuvenation.
- ☐ Wisdom.
- ☐ Knowledge.
- ☐ Growth.
- ☐ Regrafting.
- ☐ Understanding.
- ☐ Power.
- ☐ Authority.
- ☐ Unity.
- ☐ Interconnection.

The most intriguing aspects of one's Internal Paradise, Creative Mindset, or Creative Playbook are determined by what is flowing through it. So, my question is, 'What is flowing through you?' 'Do you know?' 'Do you even care?' If you do, let us get the Spiritual Ammunition needed to propitiate God, *As It Pleases Him*.

Why must we appease God? He is the Creator of all things, including you! If you think for a minute that you can appease yourself and inherit the Kingdom of God with Him nowhere in the equation, deception is knocking on your back door. No pun intended; let us take it to the Word of God. *"The word of the Lord also came to me, saying, Son of man, you dwell in the midst of a rebellious house, which has eyes to see but does not see, and ears to hear but does not hear; for they are a rebellious house."* Ezekiel 12:1-2.

The bottom line is that either you play by your rules to get what you want, or you can play by God's Rules and get what He has for you. Just know this when deciding: Rebellion is what got us into this mess, and it is going to take obedience to get us out of it.

In the Creative Playbook, here is the Spiritual Seal to use with the Four Rivers Principles and the Tree of Life: *"But now, thus says the Lord, who created you, O Jacob, And He who formed you, O Israel: Fear not, for I have redeemed you; I have called you by your name; You are Mine. When you pass through the waters, I will be with you; And through the rivers, they shall not overflow you. When you walk through the fire, you shall not be burned, nor shall the flame scorch you."* Isaiah 43:1-2.

Spiritual Ammunition

The power hidden within our Spiritual Ammunition, *As It Pleases God*, has a penetrating force that will put our enemies to boot. Whether the enemy is within us, around us, or hidden behind a bushel waiting to launch an attack, our Spiritual Ammunition will do what it is designed to do when we MASTER how to use it.

When we speak about ammunition, we often think about it negatively. But when we embrace Spiritual Ammunition, *As It Pleases God*, it takes on a whole new trajectory.

In the Creative Playbook and when dealing with a Creative Mindset, *As It Pleases God*, our Spiritual ammunition covers a wide range of Spiritual Tools and Divine Resources. When using them correctly, they enable us to navigate through the Vicissitudes and Cycles of Life with courage, tenacity, wisdom, and resilience. Here is a list of Spiritual Ammunition, but not limited to such:

- *Spirit to Spirit* Communion with God.
- Spiritual Principles and Laws.
- Prayer.
- Fasting.
- Repenting.
- Forgiveness.
- Meditation.
- Word of God.
- Positive Affirmations.
- Fruits of the Spirit.
- Gratefulness.
- The Holy Spirit.
- The Blood of Jesus.
- Truthfulness.
- Humility.
- Obedience.
- Gratitude.
- Authenticity.
- Righteousness.
- Spiritual Gifts.
- Predestined Blueprint.
- Divine Purpose.
- Positive action.
- Faith, hope, and love.
- Courage and resilience.
- Compassion, empathy, and kindness.
- A commitment to lifelong learning.
- Testaments and Testimonies.

Our Spiritual Weapons are intended to fortify the Mind, Body, Soul, and Spirit, inspiring positive and selfless action.

However, some of them may not appear like Spiritual Tools or Weapons, but rather, they are qualities, practices, and mindsets that contribute to our growth and well-being.

When our Spiritual Ammunition is used properly, and *As It Pleases God*, it becomes POWERFUL when activated or set in motion to heal, uplift, and unite. On the other hand, when selfish desires or destructive intentions drive us to divide, degrade, or harm, we will disarm ourselves from our Spiritual Covering.

Why would we lose our Spiritual Covering as Believers? There are many reasons we can lose our Spiritual Covering. However, here is a list of a few reasons, but not limited to such:

- ☐ Disobedience and rebellion.
- ☐ Debauchery and lying.
- ☐ Engaging in what God hates.
- ☐ Straying away from God to please ourselves.
- ☐ Lacking humility and beginning to play god.
- ☐ Pimping God for the benefits.
- ☐ The lust of the eyes.
- ☐ The lust of the flesh.
- ☐ The pride of life.
- ☐ Not using the Fruits of the Spirit.
- ☐ Blaspheming the Holy Spirit.
- ☐ Misusing the Blood of Jesus.
- ☐ Praying amissly to curse people.
- ☐ Wishing ill will on the innocent.
- ☐ Uncontrollable tongue.
- ☐ Negative and chaotic environments.
- ☐ Unresolved trauma or initiating trauma.
- ☐ Toxic relationships and harmful influences.
- ☐ Unforgiveness and resentment.
- ☐ Judgment and intolerance.
- ☐ Misuse of power, status, and influence.

- [ ] Mental, Physical, Emotional, and Spiritual abuse.

Then again, life's distractions and demands of everyday life can lead us astray without knowing it. However, it is our responsibility to reconnect with God, address our issues, overcome our challenges with selflessness, use our Spiritual Ammunition for the Greater Good, grow from our experiences, and emerge better, stronger, and wiser.

With our Spiritual Ammunition, it is essential to approach the activation of God's Divine Presence with humility, respect, empathy, gratefulness, and a commitment to fostering a positive and uplifting *Spirit to Spirit* Connection. Here are a few ways to positively or negatively activate God to avoid misconstruing His Divine Presence, but not limited to such:

- [ ] We can activate through our words.
- [ ] We can activate through our thoughts.
- [ ] We can activate through our actions.
- [ ] We can activate through our beliefs.
- [ ] We can activate through our mindsets.
- [ ] We can activate through our heart postures.
- [ ] We can activate through our fruits.
- [ ] We can activate through our character.
- [ ] We can activate through our faith.
- [ ] We can activate through our humility or pompousness.
- [ ] We can activate through our righteousness or unrighteousness.
- [ ] We can activate through our obedience or disobedience.

Once again, all these can be activated positively or negatively. Suppose we desire to embrace the Creative Mindset. In this case, it is imperative to channel our innermost thoughts, desires, emotions, and experiences into some form of artistry, music, writing, or some form of creative expression to turn our normal passion into Divine Passion. *"Therefore we do not lose heart. Even though our outward man is perishing, yet the inward man is being renewed day by day."* 2 Corinthians 4:16.

Using our Spiritual Ammunition reminds me of the Biblical account of the Walls of Jericho coming down in Joshua 6:1-20. In my opinion, this is a powerful demonstration of faith, obedience, and Divine Intervention. The Israelites, led by Joshua, encircled the city once a day for six days. On the seventh day, they marched around the city seven times before the walls miraculously collapsed after the army gave a mighty shout, and as the priests blew their trumpets as instructed by God. This incredible event serves as a TESTAMENT to the unwavering faith of the Israelites and the extraordinary power of God.

"Now Joshua had commanded the people, saying, 'You shall not shout or make any noise with your voice, nor shall a word proceed out of your mouth, until the day I say to you, 'Shout!' Then you shall shout.'" Joshua 6:10. So let us go deeper in closing the Creative Mindset, *As It Pleases God* to march around your personal Wall of Jericho as you Zip Your Lips to possess what rightly belongs to you!

Zip Your Lips

The power of our Spiritual Ammunition is predicated on knowing when to Unzip or Zip our Lips. Why is power there? The power is hidden in using our inside voices. When speaking to our Heavenly Father, *Spirit to Spirit*, it develops our connectivity and our inside voice, knowing when to vocalize or silence it.

What is silentize? The act of being silent but not unheard. In all simplicity, silencing our language in the Earthly Realm does not mean that it is not heard in the Heavenly Realm. The goal is to develop our inside voices, *As It Pleases God*, to maximize our Heaven on Earth Experiences without showing our hands too quickly.

What is our inside voice? We often hear the phrase 'use your inside voice' as a reminder to speak softly, kindly, and respectfully in certain environments or around certain people. Similarly, when we communicate *Spirit to Spirit* with God, it is important to approach Him with reverence, precision, and humility, using our 'inside voice' both literally and metaphorically.

Often enough, we are taught to be loud, bodacious, and demanding to be heard by God, but it is the opposite of that! Blasphemy, right? Wrong. *"And when you pray, do not use vain repetitions as the heathen do. For they think that they will be heard for their many words. Therefore, do not be like them. For your Father knows the things you have need of before you ask Him."* Matthew 6:7-8.

Using our inside voices with God to spark our Creative Mindsets or Creative Playbook begins with the practice of silence. We must hear and understand what is going on between our two ears without drowning our words, thoughts, and petitions with the power-draining loudness as if God cannot hear us. *"Before a word is on my tongue you, Lord, know it completely."* Psalm 139:4.

For the record, if you cannot sit still by yourself and with your own thoughts, there is a big problem. What type of problem? You have too much ungoverned chatter going on, preventing you from hearing, seeing, or understanding God properly. Who am I to judge since I am not in your head, right? No judgment intended, but when God is doing His handiwork of positioning, purging, and inviting, this is what is required of you: *"Be silent in the presence of the Lord GOD; For the day of the LORD is at hand, For the LORD has prepared a sacrifice; He has invited His guests."* Zephaniah 1:7.

In the midst of our busy and noisy lives, contending with the hustle and bustle of the real world, finding moments of quiet reflection allows us to connect with God, *Spirit to Spirit*. Whether through prayer, meditation, or simply being still, silence creates a SACRED SPACE for us to listen to God's Divine Voice and Guidance. Plus, when our mouths are wide open, begging, demanding, and ordering Him around, we will miss the Divine Message and Spiritual Discernment. *"For the pagans run after all these things, and your heavenly Father knows that you need them."* Matthew 6:32.

Why can we not discern properly as Believers? Our Spiritual Discerning faculties or Spiritual Compass is keeled or cloudy and lacks the *Spirit to Spirit* Connection, *As It Pleases God*. Then again, if we do not use the Fruits of the Spirit, our character traits or unrepentant rotten fruits can prevent us from hearing properly due to selfishness, pompousness, disobedience, or the misuse of what we discern. What does this mean? If we are not using the Fruits of the Spirit, our Spiritual Discernment will become thwarted or untrustworthy due to one's heart posture.

For example, the loudest person in the room, who appears to be strong in the eyes of men, is actually weak in the Eye of God. Meanwhile, it is the quiet ones who know who they are, why they are, where they are, how they came to be, and with whom they serve that we need to worry about.

Why would we need to worry when they cannot open their mouths, communicate, or articulate properly? Most often, they are speaking, but we just cannot hear or monitor them because they are using their inside voice. Above all, when they sound their trumpets to the Heavenly of Heavens, the Walls of Jericho, or whatever they are dealing with, will come down or yield the lessons needed to make them better, stronger, or wiser.

According to the Heavenly of Heavens, we should spend more time listening and documenting to keep the psyche from selfishly demanding God like He is our puppet or a pauper. The moment we get to the point as if we are running the show, rest assured, the rug will be pulled Mentally, Physically, Emotionally, or Spiritually. So, it is always best to honor Him with humility, gratefulness, and respect. Plus, a deep sense of gratitude and worship *Spirit to Spirit* will do what needs to be done, shifting our focus from our worries, doubts, and concerns to the mindset of being Blessed to be a Blessing.

Using one's inside voice with God encompasses silence, honest communication, respect, humility, listening, documenting, and a whole bunch of gratitude. With this approach, *As It Pleases Him*, our Spiritual Discernment will come forth accurately. How? Our Spiritual Discernment amplifies our Spiritual Power in conjunction with our ZIPPED LIPS in the waiting process. Is this Biblical? I would have it no other way. *"He gives power to the weak, And to those who have no might He increases strength. Even the youths shall faint and be weary, And the young men shall utterly fall, But those who wait on the Lord shall renew their strength; They shall mount up with wings like eagles, They shall run and not be weary, They shall walk and not faint."* Isaiah 40:29-31.

In our Creative Playbook, we must learn how to zip our lips, knowing when to speak and when to plead the 5th and move forward in the Spirit of Excellence.

Why should we move forward in silence when developing a Creative Mindset? The first Spiritual Principle in Zipping Your Lips is that it preserves the soul of mankind. *"Whoever guards his mouth and tongue keeps his soul from troubles."* Proverbs 21:23.

The second Spiritual Principle in Zipping Your Lips is that it preserves your life. *"He who guards his mouth preserves his life, but he who opens wide his lips shall have destruction."* Proverbs 13:3.

The third Spiritual Principle in Zipping Your Lips is that it severs you from a deceptive mindset associated with the unbridling of your tongue. *"If anyone among you thinks he is religious, and does not bridle his tongue but deceives his own heart, this one's religion is useless."* James 1:26.

The fourth Spiritual Principle in Zipping Your Lips is that it determines whether you are a Tree of Life or a Tree of Death. *"A wholesome tongue is a tree of life, but perverseness in it breaks the spirit."* Proverbs 15:4.

The last Spiritual Principle in Zipping Your Lips is that it helps you with your accountability for yourself and others while being about your Father's Business. *"But I say to you that for every idle word men may speak, they will give account of it in the day of judgment."* Matthew 12:36.

When moving forward with the Holy Trinity at the forefront, we will get dizzy with our mouths wide open. Thus, when moving forward in the Spirit of Excellence, we cannot operate with loose lips when we are confronted until the time is right.

Why do we not have the freedom to say whatever, whenever, however, and to whomever? Oh, but we do have free will. Still, we all know that loose lips sink ships, and open mouths get fed whatever, especially when greed is involved. Contrarily, in the Kingdom, Zipped lips build ships, and closed mouths get rejuvenation from manna (Heavenly Nourishment). All we need to do is ask with our inside voice, 'What Is It?' and 'Who sent you?'

According to the Heavenly of Heavens, an undisciplined tongue will place us in a Spiritually Unusable category in the Realm of the Spirit. Why do we become unusable as Believers? Because we should already know that we do not need to respond to everything or everyone, especially when it is negative, provoking, degrading, biased, or entrapping. Furthermore, we are required to move in the Spirit of Excellence, not in the Spirit of Debauchery.

In a world where opinions are rampant and social media platforms are constantly buzzing with activity, it can be tempting to respond to everything and everyone. However, our Creative Playbook teaches us the importance of knowing when to speak and when to plead the 5th.

According to the Heavenly of Heavens, we must learn to recognize or discern when a response is necessary and when it is best to remain silent. Why must we learn how to discern the difference? Popping off will not get us any brownie points in the Kingdom. Actually, it causes us to get a Spiritual Side-Eye from our Heavenly Father due to the lack of self-control or emotional intelligence, as it involves being aware of our own emotions and those of others.

Why do we need emotional intelligence as Believers? Emotional intelligence can help us navigate difficult situations and maintain positive relationships. It involves being mindful of our own reactions and the impact they may have on others, and being able to regulate our emotions healthily.

Developing emotional intelligence can be a valuable tool for anyone, especially those working in creative fields where collaboration and communication are essential in regulating our people skills. Here are a few things to avoid doing, but not limited to such:

- ☐ We do not want to escalate a situation.
- ☐ We do not want to create unnecessary tension.
- ☐ We do not want to waste our time and energy.
- ☐ We do not want to engage in unfruitful arguments or debates.
- ☐ We do not want to sling dirt that serves no purpose.
- ☐ We do not want to cause more harm than good.
- ☐ We do not want to allow negativity to fester.
- ☐ We do not want to cause willful trauma.
- ☐ We do not want to instigate chaos and confusion.
- ☐ We do not want to mock ourselves or others.

Moreover, when pleading the 5th, we are not necessarily admitting guilt, frailty, wrongness, or weakness. Instead, it is a way of exuding self-control and protecting ourselves from the creative work or entrapments of the enemy. Sometimes, it is better to remain silent and let our positive actions and reinforcements speak for themselves. What does this mean? If we want our Spiritual Ammunition to work, *As It Pleases God*, we must use the Fruits of the Spirit and behave Christlike to ensure we do not stub our own toes when misbehaving.

Above all, when maximizing emotional intelligence, *As It Pleases God*, we are better able to embark on mental intelligence and contribute to the Creative Mindset from the Heavenly of Heavens. Here are a few questions to ask ourselves when we are in doubt about something or someone, but not limited to such:

- ☐ Is God disappointed when we do not treat others with kindness and compassion?
- ☐ Does God frown upon our selfish or greedy actions?
- ☐ How does God feel when we harm the environment?
- ☐ Is God displeased when we neglect our responsibilities?
- ☐ Does God frown upon acts of hatred and violence?
- ☐ How does God view our lack of empathy toward others?
- ☐ Is God disappointed when we fail to live up to our full potential?
- ☐ Does God frown upon dishonesty and deceit?
- ☐ How does God feel about our failure to show gratitude?
- ☐ Is God displeased when we ignore the needs of the less fortunate?
- ☐ Does God frown upon our lack of forgiveness towards others?

- ☐ How does God view our failure to seek justice for the oppressed?
- ☐ Is God disappointed when we neglect our Spiritual Well-Being?
- ☐ Does God frown upon our arrogance and pride?
- ☐ How does God feel about our failure to show love and compassion towards others?
- ☐ Is God displeased when we prioritize material possessions over Spiritual Growth?
- ☐ Does God frown upon our failure to live in harmony with others?
- ☐ How does God view our lack of effort in making the world a better place?
- ☐ Is God disappointed when we stray from our moral principles?
- ☐ Does God frown upon our failure to appreciate the beauty of CREATION?

What is the purpose of asking ourselves these questions? They get our mental wheels turning on how to query God in our *Spirit to Spirit* alone time with Him. If we ask the question, wait for the answer quietly, and document the answer when received. What if we do not get an answer? Then, move to the next question.

If you follow the instructions in this book, He will answer some of these questions to develop your Spiritual Ears to hear. So, *"Be anxious for nothing, but in everything by prayer and supplication, with thanksgiving, let your requests be made known to God."* Philippians 4:6.

Will God really develop our Spiritual Ears to hear with this book? Absolutely. He developed my Spiritual Ears to hear Him clearly, enabling me to document accordingly, *Spirit to Spirit*. And, with your obedience and willingness, He will develop yours to receive according to your Predestined

Blueprinted Mission. Above all, you have free will to TEST the Spirit to see if this book is for you...I do not mind.

Why do I not mind being tested? I am a mere Messenger...what is for you will be, and what is not for you will never be. Plus, the only way that I can bring forth such Divine Revelations is to be thoroughly TESTED from the Heavenly of Heavens. So, being tested by men can never compare to what I have endured to be CHOSEN to do what I do.

With your newly refreshed Creative Mindset, and when making your Creative Playbook work on your behalf, make sure of this: *"Therefore, putting away lying, 'Let each one of you speak truth with his neighbor,' for we are members of one another. 'Be angry, and do not sin': do not let the sun go down on your wrath, nor give place to the devil."* Ephesians 4:25-27.

The timeless wisdom of Apostle Paul has a way of transforming us in ways that boggle our minds if we dare to shed our old ways intentionally. Here is what Ephesians 4:22-24 says, *"That you put off, concerning your former conduct, the old man which grows corrupt according to the deceitful lusts, and be renewed in the spirit of your mind, and that you put on the new man which was created according to God, in true righteousness and holiness."* In essence, here is what we need to focus on with a heart transformation, *As It Pleases God*:

- ☐ Put away old things or the past.
- ☐ Renew your mind.
- ☐ Embrace the new.
- ☐ Embrace True Righteousness and Holiness.

For a time such as this, and according to the Ancient of Days, our ethical conduct and the power of positive speech are on the Divine Agenda. Therefore, with a Creative Mindset, we are required to represent the Kingdom of God with the Spiritual Etiquette from the Heavenly of Heavens.

In conclusion, you now have the Spiritual Blueprint handed to you on a Silver Platter. Dig your heels in and get to work; your Divine Destiny awaits you. Grow Great...I believe in you! And, "Let him who stole steal no longer, but rather let him labor, working with his hands what is good, that he may have something to give him who has need. Let no corrupt word proceed out of your mouth, but what is good for necessary edification, that it may impart grace to the hearers." Ephesians 4:28-29.

Dr. Y. Bur

www.DrYBur.com

www.ingramcontent.com/pod-product-compliance
Lightning Source LLC
Chambersburg PA
CBHW071715160426
43195CB00012B/1690